THE STEWARDSHIP OF EXECUTIVE MANAGEMENT

FOR THE MANAGER WHO MANAGES MANAGERS

A Primer for the Newly Appointed Executive

A Refresher for the Veteran

Book 1 in the Stewardship of management Series

Like a ship at sea, an organization will accomplish its mission or founder, depending on how it is managed.

Lawrence Wade Johnson

14060606

The Stewardship
Of Executive Management

For the Manager who Manages Managers

A Primer for the New Executive, a Refresher for the Veteran

The world of top-level management belongs to the bold. As every successful manager knows, rewards are granted for results not for effort.

Executive Managers are the stewards of the organization's resources, the natural custodians of its stability, its reputation, its methods, and its future. The chief executive is the chief steward.

ISBN 1-4196-9577-0

ISBN 9781419695773

© 1987 Lawrence Wade Johnson

©1999 Lawrence Wade Johnson

©2007 Lawrence Wade Johnson

All rights reserved   December 2010

Raven Publications
Clinton, Tennessee 37717

Acknowledgements

I am indebted to those who read the manuscript and provided me with the benefit of their thinking regarding the delivery method, the believability of the case study, the connection of the case study to the management assessments and the value of the management philosophy I used in the executive assessments.

Captain Ron Eslinger, MS., USN retired

Captain Harold D. Oshucha, MA. USN retired

Colonel Gary Goff Ph.D., US Army Special Forces retired

    President Roane State Community College

Joseph Lay, CEO Lay Meat Packing Corporation

Paul Phillips Ed.D. Former Assistant School Superintendent, Dade County Florida School System

My very special thanks to:

Commander Bruce Bevard, USNR-R Nuclear Submarine Officer

I also want to thank these fine folks.

Bruce Horne, Ph.D.

David Truan

Cindy Van Sandt

Jutta Bangs

Phyllis March

Chris Parton

Chris "Gray Wolf" Olka

Cover design by Steve Sharp (steve_sharp@comcast.net)

To my shipmates
I took some license for the benefit of the story.
You will see them.
I know better!
Cut me some slack!

USS WARREN LYNN CARD (DE 383) is a fictitious ship. The officers and crew are also fictitious. The model for the ship used in this work was taken from two ships on which I served: USS Mills (DER-383) an *Edsall*-class Destroyer Escort, and the USS Roberts (DE 749) a *Cannon*-class Destroyer Escort, both were built for the United States Navy near the end of World War II.

Quite some time back, the Department of Defense decided that reserve units should be able to join the active duty forces without delays for extensive upgrading and training. Consequently both the Captain and the Executive Officer are full-time active duty officers rather than participating in the management of the ship only on weekends or other occasions. I felt the story didn't work as well the new way, so I retained the former arrangement.

The story takes place from December 1969 to the late summer of 1970. Women were not assigned to ships until the late 1990's but I included them in the story in order to bring a wider perspective to the story line.

The book is formatted as a case study. At the end of each chapter I provide the benefit of my thinking. Regarding the events that occurred and compare them with real life experiences I have had with client organizations and the outcomes of those interventions. Each assessment ends with management axioms I have collected over the years and Wade Johnson's "Rules of Command."

Respectfully,

Wade Johnson

Preface

USS WARREN LYNN CARD (DE 383) is a fictitious ship. The model for the ship used in this work was taken from two ships on which I served; USS Mills (DE-383) an *Edsall*-class destroyer escort built for the U.S. Navy during World War II, and the USS Roberts (DE 749) a *Cannon*-class destroyer escort also built for the United States Navy during World War II. The officers and crew are also fictitious. The events depicted in the case study are based on real events the author has witnessed first-hand. They actually occurred but in different organizations at different times. Captain Mills and Lieutenant Winthrop are composite characters based on four senior executives with whom I have worked. The methods used to handle the described situations were the actual methods used by these experienced top managers. The other officers and crew mentioned are also composite characters.

Why a ship? A ship is an excellent composite organization. Like a self-contained ship at sea, organizations reach their objective, or fail, depending on how the combined technical and interpersonal skills of its people are utilized. The story of the ship is simply the framework around which I have built the workshop. Why a U.S. Naval Reserve Force Ship? The military provides a clearly defined operational organization and unity of command. The members of such an organization could be less homogeneous; I could ascribe to them a wider variety of motives, intensity and involvement for the purposes of analysis and discussion.

Quite some time back, the Department of Defense decided that reserve units should be able to join the active duty forces without delays for extensive upgrading and training consequently both the Captain and the Executive Officer are now on full-time active duty rather than participating in the management of the ship only on weekends or other occasions. I felt the seminar using the Card didn't work as well the new way, so I retained the former arrangement.

The selected content is somewhat arbitrary and by no means covers all areas of leadership and management. While we can isolate the various elements that make up leadership and management such as planning, organizing, directing, controlling, discipline and morale, etc., etc., they are all fingers on the same hand, and must all work together if effective managerial activity is to take place.

The factors examined in this work are timeless. Human nature does not change as the centuries go by, thus the management of human beings does not change as well. The story takes place in the early 1970's. Women were not assigned to ships until the late 1990's but I included them in the story since the management of human beings in the work place has included women since the late 1920's.

The Stewardship of Executive Management

A Management Primer for the Manager who Manages Managers

To my shipmates	7
Preface	9
Chapter 1 – Hoisting the Flag - Assessing the Organization	13
Chapter 1 - Executive Assessment – Identifying the Organization	
• Setting the Course - Establishing Presence	
• Vision, Culture & Tradition	33
• Change of Command	
• The Turn Around Project	
Chapter 2 – Storm Warnings	42
Chapter 2 – Executive Assessment Storm Warnings	50
• Attitudes, Job Satisfaction, Compliance and Cooperation	50
• Morale, Motivation & Discipline, – Running a tight ship	55
Chapter 3 - Collision Course	59
Chapter 3 Executive Assessment -Collision Course	70
• Challenges to Authority	70
• Earning Respect and Status	72
• Controlling Operations	73
Chapter 4 - General Quarters - Battle Stations	77
Chapter 4 - Executive Assessment - Battle Stations	90
• Leadership, Stewardship, management and command	90
• Power, Authority & Politics	96
Chapter 5 - Battle Condition X-Ray	103
Chapter 5 - Executive Assessment Battle Condition X-Ray	107
• Contracting for Outside Services	107
Chapter 6 - S.O.S	115
Chapter 6 Executive Assessment S.O.S	119
• Handling disappointment, criticism and defeat	119
Chapter 7 - Flank Speed	127
Chapter 7 Executive Assessment –Flank Speed	135
• Organizational Development	135
• Training and Development	137
• Passing the Conn – Management Succession	141
• Evaluating the Performance of Subordinate Managers	144
• What To Do with Executives who Are No Longer Effective	

Chapter 8 Steady As She Goes	151
Chapter 8 Executive Assessment – Steady As She Goes	159
• Learning at the Feet of the Masters	159
• Handling Talent and Temperament	164
Postlude	165
Wade Johnson's 14 rules of command	167
Post Script	169
The Captain	169
US Navy glossary	171

Chapter 1
Hoisting the Flag - Assessing The Organization
Monday, 05 January 1970
Senior Officer's Dining Room
Officer's Club, Washington, D.C.

0700: Captain Bernard "Buck" Sorenson was a tall man, in his late fifties. He had a full head of gray and white hair, and looked every bit of a seasoned naval officer having experienced many years at sea and the weight of command. He wore his tailor-made uniform smartly and with pride. This uniform never knew a wrinkle, and every item on his dark blue jacket was in its proper place.

He had been friends with Commander Robert Mills for several years, having served as his commanding officer on the Destroyer *Mayfield,* then employing him for several assignments when he was the fleet commander for Naval Organizational Development Services. For the past year he had carried the mantel of Commander Reserve Destroyer Squadron 34. He asked Commander Mills to meet him for breakfast to seek his help with a real problem that needed expert organizational assessment, development and renewal skills, and a great resource of finesse coupled with hard-nosed persistence.

Mills was a commanding type of man. He stood 5'11" but appeared much taller with his erect way of walking, shoulders back and chin out. He had the military bearing of a senior officer. He was clean and athletic looking. Holding his hat in his left hand tucked up under his arm between his elbow and ribs, only a glimpse of the gold hatband and officers' crest could be seen. His arm all but covered the gold braid on the bill of his cap only inches away from the three gold strips on the bottom of his Navy blue sleeve which identified him as a full commander.

Commander Mills was a reserve officer with most of his sixteen years in the Navy on sea duty with several Destroyers and Destroyer Escorts. Robert Mills transferred from the regular navy to the ready reserves to take up the family business. Now his primary function was the CEO and principal of a corporation he inherited from his father and uncle, known as *The Benchmark Group* in Silver Spring Maryland. His father and uncle were killed when their corporate plane went down over Delaware, leaving a thriving three generation "turn-around" consulting firm without leadership. On the plane also was Robert Mills' wife. She was a last minute pickup. The corporate plane was flying from Boston and stopped at JFK airport to rescue Elizabeth Mills who had missed her plane after her conference ran late. Two years has passed, and he still grieves for his uncle and father, but most of all he grieves for his beloved wife. There is picture of her on his night stand, one in his wallet and two pasted to the instrument panel of his personal car.

His first assignment with *The Benchmark Group* was for the Navy. He was contracted to several squadron and battle group commanders, to implement a new operational protocol directed toward a more cooperative battle management procedure. The project required a great resource of finesse coupled with hard-nosed persistence.

This assignment was followed by other organizational development activities on board several regular navy ships.

Commander Mills was the go-to guy when an organization was in trouble and having difficulty in maintaining performance standards.

Captain Sorenson stood up from the table to greet his guest as Commander Mills approached. Holding his napkin in his left hand, he extended his right hand to receive the commander's handshake.

"Glad to see you Bob," he said. He pointed to the chair across from him as he was returning to his chair. "Sit down my boy, sit down. I am glad you got here early."

"You know me, Captain I try to be a little early."

The waiter stood at attention at the table and took their orders. They both ordered steak and eggs, toast and coffee.

When the waiter was out of earshot, the Captain leaned forward. "Let's get right to it Bob. I have a real dilly of a problem this time, and I need my top man on it. And you know that would be you."

"I hope I can help."

"This is a very top-level situation, and it will be observed by the top brass in the Navy. A lot is riding on a successful outcome of this project. I don't mind telling you my career will be greatly influenced by the outcome, and if you will accept the assignment, so will yours . . . Negatively, if it doesn't work out, and very positively if it does."

"I am intrigued. What is the assignment?"

Without taking his eyes from his friend across the table the old Captain reached down for the brief case he had stationed next to his chair. The locks had been opened for easy access when the time came. He lifted a manila folder and placed it on the table in front of him. He spun it around so the bottom of the folder was facing the direction of the Commander. Commander Mills noticed the U.S. Navy logo imprinted on the cover. Just under the seal in block stencil letters was: *Commander Reserve Destroyer Squadron 34 Special Orders.*

The Captain's eyes shifted from his guest to the sugar container and the salt and pepper shakers in the middle of the table, and he moved them to the port side. Then, focusing on the folder, he slid it toward Commander Mills. With his fingers resting on the mysterious package he looked into the Commander's face.

"I hope you will agree to take this assignment for me, Bob." He withdrew his hand from the folder.

Without lifting the folder the Commander opened the cover. He said nothing for a minute or so, just staring at the paper inside.

The waiter came over with two gold rimmed white cups that bore gold insignia spelling out *Officers Club USN Washington DC*. Commander Mills closed the cover and paused as the waiter poured the coffee. He used a gold rimmed white china plate as a splash guard between the target cup and each officer as he poured coffee from a silver plated coffee pot with an "S" shaped spout.

Having completed that, he wiped the spout with a napkin, collected the splash plate, and walked away. Commander Mills opened the folder cover and again read the paper.

To: Robert Mills CDR USNR-R
From: Commander Reserve Destroyer Squadron 34
Date: 09 January, 1970
Unclassified: Orders to command

You will assume command of USS WARREN LYNN CARD (DE 383) on 13 February, 1970. The ship and its officers and crew are to be brought up to combat readiness and join Reserve Destroyer Squadron 34 for combat readiness-evaluation exercises at Guantanamo Bay, Cuba during the period 21 July through 3 August 1970.

Bernard "Buck" Sorenson
Captain USN
ComResDesRon 34 Commanding

The Commander looked up from the paper at his old friend and boss. There was more to this than just a command. Captain Sorenson tried to read his expression. Mills seemed to be in doubt as to whether to accept the assignment, he thought. "The *Card* is tied up at the Coast Guard Yard at Curtis Bay in Baltimore, not an hour's drive from your office in Silver Springs."

"You realize Captain that I have not had actual command of a naval vessel, of any size. Why me, and why this ship?"

"I know, Bob. This is not just an assignment to command a reserve force vessel. The *Card* is in too poor condition to assign to just any senior officer to Captain the ship. I need a turn-around expert, one who knows how to save lost causes and the one person for that task is Commander Robert Mills." He looked into his friend's eyes. The old salt was worried, and Robert Mills could see it.

"It is a sick ship, and needs a Captain, who can turn around bad situations . . . a person with peripheral awareness, and the ability to instill vision, hope and purpose into an operation. But it needs to be a person with people skills as well."

"You said top brass is interested in this ship, why?"

"Well, it is not functioning. It has strategic value to the nation. As you know, all naval vessels, including reserve ships have a secret mission they must carry out in the event the US is under destructive assault.

If that was not enough it is under my command, ComResDesRon 34, and I am responsible for it."

"Is there a political element to this ship?"

Captain Sorenson hesitated before answering. His voice went low. "OK. Yes . . . there is . . . there is a Winthrop aboard and he has become a bit of a disappointment to the Naval Winthrops."

"Tell me more."
Captain Sorenson had hoped his friend would jump at a chance to command a ship; most senior officers would. But there was no finessing the issue with this man. He had to be brutally blunt.

"Captain William Footsellers Gallagher, a full Bird four striper, was scheduled to retire in January of last year, but I convinced him to take custody of the *Card* until a suitable Captain could be appointed. An investigation of the daily operations of the *Card* seems to show that Captain Gallagher had only nominally been in command of the ship, almost managing by abdication."

"Hmm," said Mills. "Nothing new so far."

"Three months after Lieutenant Winthrop reported aboard," Sorenson continued, "Captain Gallagher officially retired. Why the sudden decision to leave now, no one knows for sure. The ship has been without a legitimate Commanding Officer since 01 July of last year. We know that Captain Gallagher was at one time a competent chief executive who was responsible for the successful careers of many young naval officers under his mentorship."

Robert Mills said nothing but continued to stare in the direction of his old boss and mentor, waiting for the *real* reason to emerge.

"Mr. Winthrop's assignment to the *Card* came from on high, very high. Someone in the Winthrop family secured his assignment to the *Card* in order to be mentored by Captain William Footsellers Gallagher, a longtime friend of the Naval Winthrops. It is well known that John Winthrop was assigned to this reserve ship to be Officer in Charge as part of a "fast track" program to prepare him for command. After a few years under Captain Gallagher he was to be assigned to a deep draft ship. Instead of this being a fast track it appears it will be a deterrent to his climb up the naval ladder as is expected by all the Winthrops."

The Winthrop family was well known and well respected in the US Naval Service. They went back to the days of 1812. Every Winthrop that went into the Navy since 1901 was required to begin at the Naval Academy in Annapolis, and they all climbed the promotion ladder to Admirals. They all began on small vessels, then on to deep draft vessels, then to command status. Those Winthrops who did not enter the naval service had big jobs and great clout in the Navy Department. These were not people you crossed . . . these were not people you disappointed. Robert Mills saw the real problem behind the *USS Card's* need for a Captain, and the real reason for the trepidation that shone on the face of his former commander.

Two waiters brought the breakfast orders. No more was said until the plates had been distributed and the napkins properly placed,

"Will you take the job Bob?"

"I can see you are in heavy seas, Buck. Give me any information you have on the *Card*, and I will do some digging myself. There is great risk in this assignment as I can see you are well aware."

The old skipper nodded his head, and then slowly shook his head sideways. "Heavy seas . . . Beauford 8." He leaned forward. "The ship and her crew need a Captain, Bob. They a need a Captain who can give them back their self-esteem, return them to the Navy. They need a Captain with a unique set of skills, the ability to establish and maintain discipline inculcated with people skills."

He reached again into his brief case and withdrew another folder. This one was fat with papers, many with colored *sticky* markers indicating important information.

"Here is all the information I collected on the ship. This should be enough information for you to make a decision." Captain Sorenson lifted the brief case and handed it over the table to Commander Mills. Mills took it and placed it beside his chair.

"How soon do you need an answer?"

The Captain said nothing he just looked forlornly at his friend, and sighed.

"I see. Well, this is Monday. Give me ten days."

"I need an answer by Monday 12 January. I have to have word to ComResDesDiv by Tuesday, 13 January and if you take the assignment I will need a need a full report and a plan no later than 19 January. I will need time to pull together a change of command."

"I wish I could visit the ship and interview the crew."

"I wish you could also, Bob, but these are unusual circumstances, what with that Winthrop guy in there."

"Let's meet for lunch here on Monday 12 January," said Mills.

"Make it breakfast."

"Breakfast then, here . . . Zero Seven Thirty . . . Monday 12 January."

"Good."

They finished their breakfast talking about general navy topics. When they finished their meal, Captain Sorenson signed for it, and they went their separate ways.

Monday, 05 January 1970
Senior Officer's Parlor
Officer's Club Washington D.C.

1100: Robert Mills retired to the lounge to read the information ComResDesRon had given him. He was greeted by a doorman who took his hat and coat. A steward dressed in a white uniform approached him and asked if he would like a drink brought to his position. He thanked him and said it would not be necessary and proceeded to the rear of the room.

He chose a position by a large window looking out over the Potomac. The center of the position was a leather wingback Queen Anne chair with a thickly padded cushion and backrest. It was oxblood burgundy, an old-fashioned chair with Button tufting on both the backrest and seat

He sat down, crossed his legs and pulled out a manila file folder marked *USS Card turnaround project; Overview.*

USS WARREN LYNN CARD (DE 383) is a fully commissioned US Navy warship, permanently assigned to the Naval Reserve Force in Reserve Destroyer Division 5 (ResDesDiv5), which is made up of Reserve Destroyer Squadron 34 (ResDesRon34) and 35 and Reserve Submarine squadron 30 (ResSubRon30).

ResDesRon34 consists of The USS Lancing, home port; Brooklyn Naval Ship Yard, USS Granger, home port; Philadelphia Naval Ship Yard, USS Card, home port; US Coast Guard Yard, Curtis Bay (Baltimore) and USS Roberts, home port Patuxent River Naval Station.

After surviving horrendous naval battles near the end of the World War 2, the Card, under competent leadership and a gallant crew, traveled the globe thereafter in defense of the nation during the Korean War and the Cold war. She took part in the Cuban Blockade in 1962. She performed in a number of roles as task group escort and anti-submarine warfare. She spent fourteen months in the North Atlantic and another six months on the ice in Antarctica and two years "steaming" around the south Pacific visiting ports as liaison representatives of the U.S. Navy.

The ships assigned to Reserve Destroyer Squadron 34, as all reserve ships, has a secret mission in case the United States comes under hostile assault. Their orders are to set sail with less than 12 hours' notice to deal with a specific task directed toward the protection of a designated part of the United States or exact revenge on an enemy for destructive action against a designated part of the U.S.

The Card's reserve crew is obligated to serve seventy-two hours one weekend each month on board for an underway sea-going training drill in preparation for their annual combat exercise at the combat training area, Guantanamo Bay Cuba ResDiv5 ships rendezvous with the rest of the destroyer squadron in Jacksonville, Florida. From there they sail into Guantanamo Bay, Cuba, for a four-day intensive combat exercise followed by three days in a Caribbean liberty port, and a five day voyage back to the home port.

After being assigned to the reserve force in 1968, the Card has suffered ignominiously from neglect more than most reserve ships due to incompetent leadership and a crew that saw itself as "Part-timers" serving one weekend a month collecting retirement points. The never-ending battle against rust, equipment failure, and general deterioration has only been approached in a half-hearted manner. As a result, the Card has been unable to join the squadron for the annual combat readiness exercise the past two years.

An accumulation of equipment problems primarily in the engine room have prevented her from leaving the pier for over nine months. The Card has the worst record on station for "getting under way Navy blue the name "CARD" has been corrupted to "CARP" by the Card's own ship's company and other ships' crews – the implication being that she's only fit to wallow in the mud.

A ship of the Card's class would normally carry a crew of 10 officers and 200 enlisted personnel. Manpower shortages and the Card's dismal record combined to have her complement cut to 22 Regular navy full time enlisted who form the "Nucleus Crew" who man her every day and 88 Reserve enlisted men and 21 reserve enlisted women (131) and 10 officers including the Captain.

Of that complement, five of the officers are full-time active duty and the other five, the Captain included, are reservists. One of the regular officers serves as the Officer in Charge (OIC) and has custody of the ship when the Captain and Executive Officer are not on board, and assumes most of the day-to-day operations.

The reserve Captain must authorize all major events, purchases and movements. When the Captain assumes command, and he doesn't have to be physically on board to do so, OIC assumes duties as Navigator and Operations Officer. When the five reserves come aboard they are integrated into the operations of the ship alongside the others.

Mills replaced the Overview file in the brief case and withdrew another manila folder. The tab read Officers Fitness Reports.

Michael "Mike" McCormick *Lieutenant Commander, USNR-R, Executive Officer. He has a B.S. degree in Marketing and Real Estate Management from Texas A&M. He is rated as a very able First Officer. He is the official second-in-command and answers to the Captain during periods when the reserve crew is in possession of the ship. In the U.S. Navy the Executive Officer (XO) is the chief operating officer, the official manager responsible for the day to day operations. All department heads report to the X.O. He also filled the ASWO (Anti-Submarine Warfare Officer) officer billet. LCDR McCormick has served on the Card for two years. Prior to this assignment he served eight years on Des in the regular Navy. He shipped to the ready reserves in 1968 and assumed the XO position when the Card was assigned to the ready reserve Force. In civilian life, he is a partner in a very successful commercial real estate firm.*

Nucleus Crew Officers

John Winthrop, *Lieutenant, USN, was assigned to the Card in March of last year to serve as Officer-In-Charge (OIC) of the ship. He was graduated from the U.S. Naval Academy where he did not excel in any subject except ship navigation.*

After graduation he spent the next 19 months in Surface Warfare School, Navigation School and Anti-Submarine Warfare School. He then served an 18 month tour of duty on the USS Pennington (DE 747) as Assistant Operations Officer. He was then transferred to The USS Bristol (DE 218) where he served as the Navigator and Assistant Operations Officer for 22 months.

Robert Mills pulled a pen from inside his coat pocket and scribbled a note under John Winthrop's bio:
Lt. Winthrop is one of a long line of Naval Winthrops. His great Grandfather and his Grandfather retired as Navy Admirals, his father and uncle hold the rank of Admiral and are currently serving in the Navy. Many other family members hold high positions in the Navy Department. He appears to have considerable influence with DesDiv5 and the officers and crew of the Card.

William "Bill" Fridel, *Lieutenant USN, serves as Engineering Officer. He is a "mustang", having come up through the enlisted ranks. He entered the Navy at seventeen and spent most of his Navy career in the engine room of two steaming supply ships (ships that spend a lot of time at sea). After eleven years as an enlisted man He graduated with a degree in Naval engineering from the University of Maryland through the Navy's six year "Remote Degree" program and an eight week OCS course. After receiving his commission he was sent to the war zones serving on three different ships over a three year period. Before coming to the Card he served in a headquarters staff position for two years where, for a reason known only to the Navy Department, he was assigned to the Card to get him out of sight until his retirement. Mister. Fridel has been on the Card for one year. He is scheduled to retire in September of this year.*

Phyllis Grubaugh, *Lieutenant, USN, was assigned to the Card in February of last year. She serves as the Weapons Officer. She is rated as a good officer and is now serving her third active duty assignment. She was born and raised in a little town in Iowa. She took an academic scholarship to the University of Maryland. After entering NROTC she became obsessed with the notion of being a career naval officer serving on a ship at sea. She decided the Navy was to be her career. After receiving her degree she took the first sea billet available, and has remained in a sea-going capacity ever since. When the reserve crew is not on board, Lt. Grubaugh serves as assistant to the Officer-In-Charge, Lt. Winthrop.*

Marshall Goldsmith, *Ensign USN, was assigned to the Card in April of last year. Mister Goldsmith was appointed as the Supply Officer. That job has a myriad of responsibilities beyond just supplies and spare parts. It includes all financial matters, food storage and preparation, and the medical division.*

In addition, Ensign Goldsmith handles the ship's personnel functions. This is his first duty assignment, having graduated from Ohio State two years ago with a degree in Human Resources Development. He went into the Navy as a Personnel Officer but was assigned supplies and stores when he reported aboard the Card, since that billet was vacant.

Nick Winchester, Ensign, USN. Assigned as Damage Control Officer in July of last year. He earned a degree in mechanical engineering from a small college in Oklahoma and was accepted into Officers Candidate School where he attended sixteen weeks of concentrated courses before receiving his commission. After Surface Warfare School he was assigned to the Card. Mr. Winchester has the demanding job of training the ship's crew in damage control procedures. In addition, he is Assistant to the Deck Officer, Lt (jg) Hooper. His many requests for transfer have been denied.

Reserve Officers
Georgia Sterling, Lieutenant USNR-R. Ms. Sterling is a highly skilled Electronics Engineer. After graduating from MIT with a master's degree in cyber electronics, she served six years on active duty aboard a large destroyer tender. Her duties included Anti Submarine Warfare and Combat Information. While at her last duty assignment in the Regular Navy, she assisted a team of civilian engineers to install a complicated "combat seek and control system" in a new class of destroyers. She so impressed the civilian team they made her an employment offer she could not refuse. She joined the firm on the condition she could serve in the Navy Ready-Reserves. Since her job took her to the ComResDesRon area she was assigned to Card as the Combat Information Center (CIC) Officer where she has been for the past 13 months.

Michael Cavatini, Lieutenant Junior Grade (jg), USNR-R arrived on 30 August of last year. He is the Communications Officer, in charge of radio, the crypto unit and the signal bridge. He was assigned nine months ago, and is still trying to make sense of the mess his predecessor left him. A graduate of Auburn University with a degree in communication electronics he joined the Navy through a delayed entry program for college students in engineering who enlist while in college and receive a commission upon graduation. He is obligated to serve four years on active duty reserve and another four years on in-active reserve. He has a standing offer to join the R&D department of a large cyber operations communications firm; after fulfilling his navy obligation. Note: Lieutenant Junior Grade is equal to a first lieutenant in the Army.

Frank Hooper, Lieutenant Junior Grade (jg) USNR-R. He has been serving as the Deck Officer on the Card for the past eighteen months. In civilian life, he is a sales representative for a multi-national ship supply company. Mr. Hooper grew up around the commercial fishing trade on the coast of Maine. His father was a third generation commercial fisherman and Mr. Hooper spent his youth working as a general repair hand on one of his father's boats. He applied for an appointment to the Coast Guard Academy but when the appointment did not come through he attended the University of Maine. He received his commission through NROTC after graduating with a degree in Naval Engineering. Except for Surface Warfare School he has had only his two-year mandatory active duty experience.

He closed the folder. He needed more inside information. Normally organization assessment is done on the premises in a work study scenario which means interning a stratified sampling of the officers and crew and just observing things in each department at various times during the night and day, and keeping notes on what is discovered.

After a while a pattern will reveal itself, and then other information seems to come out of the woodwork, so to speak. But if he were to be the new Captain he had to make his first appearance an official one. He called Buck Sorenson's office and got the phone number of former skipper William Footsellers Gallagher. He made a late lunch date at the officers club for 1300 that afternoon.

The meal with Captain Gallagher was very informative and lasted two hours. After lunch Mills drove back to his office in Silver Springs, Maryland.

Friday, 09 January 1970
Office of the Benchmark Consulting Group
Silver Springs Maryland.

1800: Robert Mills wrote a summary of all he had discovered from Captain Sorenson, Captain Gallagher and the information from the files.

The ship suffers from a bad reputation. The reputation of the organization is another significant factor in morale. The perception of status in the eyes of others in the organization and outside the organization affects morale. Oddly enough their perception of the boss' status and reputation in the eyes of the higher ups is a contributing factor in the morale of the crew. Other elements include competent management and worthwhile work. Jobs have purpose and its contribution to the organization's mission is apparent. Camaraderie in the work group is a key element in morale. People need people. It is important that people in the work force regard each other with respect.

A major contribution to the problem is a bad attitude. Job performance, job behavior and military bearing of the officers and the crew is unacceptable. There is no commitment to discipline, no commitment to the mission, and no commitment to the organization. The only cooperation between departments is that necessary to maintain the status quo. There is no real job involvement.

The conduct of well-disciplined employees is the result of training that has caused them to accept and live according to certain behavior patterns. In most cases, where a person has had extensive training in some professional discipline, or a highly skilled trade, self-discipline is almost automatic when morale and motivation are present.

Since the crew is not allowed to participate in the mission of the organization, they cannot demonstrate the competence and commitment necessary to improve the reputation. They have forgotten that it is the crew that determines the organization's reputation, not the reverse.

Two major events must occur. (1) They must be allowed to perform.

The ship must get underway and they must do the jobs they were hired to do. (2) They must identify with the ship to the extent they are willing to do the jobs they were hired to do.

The crew was ashamed to identify with the ship. If they were to be proud of her they needed to identify with her and bring her up to Navy standards. To further ingrain identity they must be required to wear the ship's identity patch on the right shoulder of their white and blue uniforms.

The crew's collective minds must have a vision of what can be, and the belief that they can make it happen. They need to buy into this vision and actively participate in making it a reality. There must be a plan for focusing on being successful and not dwelling on failure. To dwell on failure will result in failure. To dwell on success will almost always result in success.

The *Card* has the worst advancement record in the Navy. This was the case for both officers and enlisted, for regular Navy and reservists. A major obstacle is the ship's limited amount of underway time. The officers and enlisted alike, are unable to perform operations which are required for advancement that could only be gotten at sea.

While three of the officers have experience "Conning" the ship, only two had ever performed the task alongside a refueling tanker. None of the enlisted helmsmen or throttle men advanced, as they should. Additionally, the lack of a concerted on-the-job training program meant that only the most dedicated and motivated of the enlisted was able to pass the examinations required for advancement. Advancement tests for sailors E-5 and above required testing while the ship was at sea. In short, the *USS Card* was a career dead-end for all assigned to her and they knew it well. The Navy's target for re-enlistment for reserve sailors was above 60%. Most ships were above 50%, but the re-enlistment rate on the *Card* hovered at around 13%.

The *USS Card's* organizational culture did not change with Captain Gallagher. It began before he took command. It began to change when the conditions required them to miss week end drills at sea and the annual combat readiness exercise. Training took a big hit also since they were not able to do simulations in underway conditions with any semblance of fidelity. The *Card's* organizational structure was adjusted to accommodate its pier-bound condition when certain officer billets and enlisted billets were discontinued.

Organizational structure greatly influences the culture because behavior is not random and is directed by some degree of formalization toward a goal, and the decisions made concerning structure contributed to the change in culture.

Captain Gallagher's decision to allow Mr. Winthrop to exercise his discretion with regard to the *Card's* condition, and Lieutenant Commander McCormick's acquiescence, simply contributed to the change in culture. The culture deteriorated into lethargy after a while, and the executive team contributed to its downward spiral by not holding itself and the crew to proper naval discipline and competence. What was worse, he had a reputation for being a "king maker," consequently the Winthrop naval dynasty relied on Footsellers Gallagher to do for the next generation of Winthrops what he had done for so many other Naval Academy protégés. But instead of passing on his great wisdom, leadership and command philosophies he allowed Mr. Winthrop to develop his own based on what he observed at the feet of the legendary naval guru.

When Lieutenant Winthrop was assigned to the *Card* as Officer-in-Charge both Captain Gallagher and Lieutenant Commander McCormick allowed him to manage not only the daily operations but also the operations of the drill weekend.

Mr. Winthrop became the center of attention the moment he set foot on the *Card*. He exerted a great deal of influence since then. In reality Mister Winthrop was the one actually in command.

After Captain Gallagher's departure, Reserve Lieutenant Commander McCormick, the ship's executive officer, assumed the role of acting Captain, but he continued to allow the officer-in-charge to call the shots even when the reserves were aboard.

The daily routine of the ship is slow and easy. Only routine work is done. Although the officers and men follow the regulation plan of the day, no major work is performed. During the drill weekend, the reservists spend most of their time doing assessments in classrooms or performing training tasks on the ship's equipment. No major repairs are undertaken except when the reserves are aboard. The crew takes liberty every night including drill weekends, although normally the drill weekend requires the crew to stay on board throughout the full 72-hour period.

Getting the ship in combat shape is only one of the objectives. The other is developing a management team that can undertake all of the rigorous activities and responsibilities necessary to achieve the ship's mission. Once the entire ship's company could accomplish something worthwhile it would be a small step to the next method of renewal.

Objective: Each department head should conduct a department assessment as a means of comparison with their department's status with combat exercise requirements followed by developing a plan to meet those requirements. When the department heads realistically examine the status of their assigned areas of responsibility they will recognize its deplorable condition and take action to correct it.

The *get well* plan must include methods for getting the crew's mind off the past and the current state of affairs and give them a vision of what can be, and the belief that they can make it happen. They need to buy into his vision and actively participate in making it a reality. The plan will provide methods for focusing on being successful and not dwelling on failure. In tandem with all that is the imperative that they get production out. The ship had stood idle too long. He must direct their attention to the task at hand. A lethargic organization does not usually realize the condition they are in until they are called on to produce to a higher standard. When the crew attempts to get the ship underway they will discover the deplorable state they are in.

Only then can the Captain begin to make corrections that will bring them to combat readiness. The crew on the *Card* may need to experience failure, before they can begin to move toward success.

For the *Card*, or any other organization to be effective, to grow, or to survive at all, it must fulfill some useful function. The common goals set by the founders of the organization must result in some product or service which is useful, and holds a certain sense of pride to those in the organization and is desired by others outside the organization.

The importance of the plan must be continually stressed. Persistence will eventually get the ship out to sea where the crew is able to see for themselves where their problems lie.

Subordinate executives must take charge of their own departments, using their own methods and leadership styles and, with his assistance, deliver the means to accomplish that objective.

Once the crew experiences the actual accomplishment of the task of being part of the team that could perform the duties of military maritime professionals on board a ship at sea, they will take on a serious attitude and renewed enthusiasm toward their job in particular and the ship in general.

Monday, 12 January 1970
Senior Officer's Dining Room
Officer's Club Washington D.C.

0730: Captain Sorenson and Commander Mills met in the senior officer's dining room at the same table where they had met previously. Mills wondered if that table was assigned to Captain Sorenson, or if he just preferred that one. He made a mental note to ask him, if the opportunity came up.

"Here is my report, Buck," he said handing over the file folder. As Buck Sorenson retrieved the folder, Commander Mills slid the brief case across the floor next to the Captain's chair. "I am pretty sure it accurately describes the situation as best it could be in such a short period of time without actually visiting the ship and interviewing the officers and crew. Even if I could, that would be out of the question, since my coming aboard as their Captain would appear like spying. The information you provided was very complete and very helpful."

"I am sure the report is well done. So you will take the assignment then?"

"Did you think I wouldn't?"

"Good! I told the big boss you would. You had me worried there for a minute, but I have known you long enough to read your face. When you heard about the politics involved you lit up. You just can't resist a challenge, not one as juicy and risky as this one."

"I will go to work as the Commanding Officer as soon as the Change of Command Ceremonies are over."

"You can start now as far as ComResDiv5 and yours truly is concerned. There is no real commander in charge over there now as it is."

"I will visit the ship as soon as I can, in an unofficial capacity and just snoop around."

"Do some recon work. Good idea. That is your specialty."

"I will need a crash course in Anti Submarine Warfare, if we are to make a good showing at the games in Gitmo. I know three of my officers are ASW qualified, but I need to show some expertise myself."

"You did some ASW work in one of your assignments for me if I recall."

"Not enough to handle myself in an engagement against a competent foe."

"Yes and you'll find competence with that submarine bunch at the games, as you so glibly call them."

They both smiled.

"I'll set you up with some experience attack team officers from SUBLANT (Submarine Atlantic Fleet) in Norfolk. We will need someone with hunter killer experience from the destroyer perspective. That kind of information is not always easy to obtain as you can well image, since those *tricks of the trade* were come by with trial and error and cognitive investment. If we are going to get some *tricks of the trade* from these guys we will need to secure those who either like you or are afraid of you."

Mills raised his eyebrows. He had not considered that element.

"Your Lieutenant Sterling," the ResDesRon boss continued, "would be one of those clever hunter killer people, if you don't mind getting instruction from a subordinate."

"I don't mind picking the brain of competent subordinates, and from I have deduced from her file, she is not only competent but brilliant and discreet."

"I'll leave that meeting up to you. Now, as far as other sources of hunter killer experts, I think Haggerty over at the Pentagon would be a good one. He taught at the ASW school and never lost a battle in Gitmo."

"Haggerty. Would that be Boise Haggerty the ASW officer on the Rodgers several years back?"

"Yes, the very one. That's right you worked with him. . . Pulled his butt out of quite a jam, as I recall it. I'll see if I can get him to meet with you." He sat back in his chair and stroked his chin, his eyes taking on a far-away look. "Hmm. Getting a crack submariner to give up some secrets of clever attack team tactics will be a tough cove to steer."

Mills sat patiently. His boss did not get where he was without ingenuity and political networking. And of course one does not make friends in high places without being a competent contributor to the network.

"I'll have to call in a favor from Dunhill. If anyone can put us onto an attack team expert, it would be him."

"Dunhill Winthrop?"

"He's our best bet. He has a stake in your assignment, what with his arrogant, ring knocker nephew on your ship in what was to be a fast track to command program going bad. When he heard I picked you to captain the *Card* he was elated. He is one of the high mucky-mucks in the Submarine Service. Let me have a go at him."

"I appreciate your help Buck."

"I'll let you know what I get for us."

They finished their meal, stood up, shook hands and went off to prepare their part in the assignment.

Saturday, 17 January 1970
USS Card Pier side
US Coast Guard Base, Curtis Bay Maryland

1700: Commander Mills decided to make an unscheduled visit to the ship in mid-January. He spent a few minutes looking at her. "She was once a magnificent vessel," he thought, "and she will be again." He admired her numbers painted in pure white with a black shadow displayed against the traditional battle ship gray. He walked down the pier and up the ships gang plank that led to the quarterdeck.

He stopped, made a brisk right face and snapped a well-executed salute to the National Ensign (American flag) flying on the fantail. Commander Mills then turned to face the quarterdeck officer and saluted. "I am Commander Robert Mills, requesting permission to come aboard." The Officer of the Deck returned his salute and said, "Permission granted."

Commander Mills stepped on to the quarterdeck. "Are you our new commanding officer?" the OOD asked.

"I will be, yes. And what is your name, mister?"

"Ensign Goldsmith, Commander."

"Well Mr. Goldsmith, I noticed that you and the quarterdeck watch are wearing a work uniform, and a foul weather jacket."

"Yes sir that is the uniform of the day for the quarterdeck."

"I want this sailor in dress blues and a pea-coat. You will stand his watch while he shifts into the proper quarterdeck uniform. When he returns, you go to your stateroom, put on a tie, Bridge Coat and gloves. Then return here in the proper uniform."

"Yes sir."

The enlisted watch departed to shift into dress blues. The new Captain had a guided tour of the ship. He left the ship after two hours.

Chapter 1 Assessment
Hoisting the Flag
Identifying the Organization and its Mission
Establishing Presence

"You only get one chance to make a first impression."

The new senior executive's first assignment is to get to know the organization, its various operations and staff units, how those units work together and, just as important, is getting to know those on the management team, their capabilities and their commitment to the organization's mission. The initial impression a newly appointed executive makes can be a lasting one and it is the time to create an environment for future actions of the organization. Under normal circumstances the new commander acknowledges the achievements the organization has experienced up to now, and expresses pride and opportunity this new command offers. The new manager in charge expresses his/her management style, philosophies, the mission of the organization, and the new manager's vision for the future.

A critical first step in any new assignment involves meeting with key subordinates. The Captain met with his subordinate managers in the wardroom immediately after the change of command ceremonies. Executives accomplish results with subordinate managers, and the sooner the senior establishes the relationship with these people, the sooner they can get down to business. The senior must alert them to his/her management style, philosophies and expectations. A new plant manager or senior executive may not have the opportunity to meet with the entire plant as the Captain did at the change of command ceremony, but everyone under the new manager's command is very interested in his or her management philosophy and what is expected. The new manager may schedule a series of meetings where the rank-and-file are provided with information regarding plans for the present and the vision for the future.

The captain looked at Personnel Records of his subordinate managers. The new manager must learn as much about his subordinates as possible in a short period. One can learn a lot from a personnel record. Personnel records are a good source of information about the person.

I have witnessed new senior executives, and plant managers assume their duties without fan fare and ceremony, they just walked in and took over in silence. Only the senior management team was privy to a meeting with the new C.O. No hourly people or second or first line managers were actually introduced. He remained a mystery, and where there is mystery there is uncertainty. I have witnessed a change of command type of activity with some organizations where they either suspended production for a day, or for an afternoon and invited all the employees to meet the new chief, hear a motivational speech and a chance to shake hands afterward.

On every occasion the new C.O.'s spouse was there to share in the program. Some organizations served food and drinks and invited the press. Some even invited the employee's families, a very nice touch, I thought.

One such event was done in the summer time outside, and other was in the fall and was catered on the production floor.

Of course these mandatory attendance programs include the hourly pay for all who attend. Many, private industry change of command ceremonies include invitations to executives in all the major industries, city and county officials (appointed and elected), and community leaders. I recommend a change of command program or at least a reception for the new chief and spouse.

The new manager can learn a lot by personally seeing the conditions under which employees must work. This personal inspection serves other worthwhile purposes, such as being a real person to those under the manager's command by speaking to them and listening to them. The new manager makes rounds and discovers first-hand the condition of the physical facilities and personnel.

Captain Mills announced; "All standing orders are to remain in effect until further notice." Usually the manager will determine the state of affairs before making major changes. The manager will discover what changes must be made right away and make plans for additional changes. People will expect some changes when new management takes over, but do not shock them by making changes before determining how they should be employed.

He did change the uniform of the day for quarterdeck watches and officers of the day in spite of the fact they were tied up to a pier so far out it practically guaranteed they would have no visitors. This action would be the first in a series of changes directed toward improving the crew's attitudes about the ship and them selves, in effect changing the organization's culture.

The Captain asked to see specific reports now and on a daily basis. The senior manager needs to know the day-to-day status of activities that directly influence the health of the organization and the accomplishment of its mission. Most senior managers have a daily briefing from department heads on the condition of operations, production and maintenance reports, schedules, receiving and shipping problems, Human Resources and special projects. Reports serve to structure attention to the organization's activities and that documentation ensures that actions taken and the status of the activities are clear.

The structure of the report offers a clear definition of the subordinate's responsibilities, clearly shows the priorities of each activity, the importance of those activities, and the expected outcome.

Reports measure, not only current status, but serve as an effective control method as it shows progress toward meeting objectives. When an activity is measured, it is tantamount to getting it accomplished. Reports also are a very important function for the newly appointed executive in the early hours of administration.

They are a means for getting subordinates used to taking orders from their new manager.

Much of the information requested by the Captain was not available a clear indication that something was dreadfully wrong.

Apparently subordinate managers did not understand the value of having detailed information regarding their area of responsibility. To bolster his project management control system the Captain reinstated the reports that the executive team had discontinued.

Captain Mills arrived at the ship unannounced allowing him to observe the operation as it really functions when not under scrutiny from an outside authority. I do not discourage this action, as a general practice. I recommend scheduling the executive's "official" arrival, but I suggest an unannounced visit the day before or several days before in order to get a true picture of the daily operations.

Management Axioms:

- Reports keep the organization on track. If a manager is not able to provide an instant report on the health and welfare of their department, they are not on top of it, something is going wrong and they don't know it. If it isn't documented, it didn't happen.
- When an activity is measured, it gets attention and gets done.

Rule of Command #1

Taking command requires getting others to think of you as the boss, and asking subordinate executives for reports regarding their departments is an intrusive but non- threatening method to accomplish that objective.

Rule of Command #2

When you are in charge, take charge.

B. Identifying the Mission

"Purposeful action begins with purpose."

The organization's mission identifies its reason for existence. The mission statement is a statement of purpose. One training and development firm issued this mission statement for its customers and employees: *Provide readily job applicable, state-of-the art computer training, effective organizational consulting, credible professional certificate exam preparation courses, operator training systems and management development courses through the use of professional adjuncts having experience and esteemed credentials.*

The mission of the organization clearly shows the organization as the goose that lays the golden eggs. As "hard-nosed" as it may seem, every member of the organization is there to assist the enterprise to accomplish its mission. Every action that takes place must benefit the organization. Every action is directed toward taking care of the goose.

When individuals come together to participate in a common objective, a mission is created and an organization is formed to accomplish that mission. The mission identifies the organization's reason for existence.

All activities that take place in the organization are directed toward the accomplishment of that mission. All production, sales & marketing efforts, manpower planning, job descriptions, training, protocols, and standard operating strategies are predicated on the organization's purpose. Any activity that does not support that is extraneous.

Each person in the organization is there for a specific purpose to do a specific job, or a set of related jobs that exist to accomplish some necessary, activity in order to help the company to satisfy its reason for existence and to stay in business. The reason any job exists is because there is a need for it. If that need disappears, the job disappears.

The organization is established to exist beyond our lifetime, and the lifetime of the chief executive and the business owners. If everyone does their job well, the organization will prosper and everyone connected with it. Everyone must show up for work when scheduled, must do their job to the best of their ability, and make a substantial contribution during the time they are on the clock.

Once a person has assumed command of a given operation, they have assumed the obligation for the pursuit of its purpose, and custody of its future, its methods, its stability and its reputation and all the resources available to accomplish the mission.

Captain Mills' was sent there to re-establish this group of officers into the team it used to be. While the officers were reluctant to buy into the chief executive's presence or whatever plan he may have brought with him, it is none-the-less true that the chief executive must establish himself as the one in charge, and insist that subordinates acknowledge that fact. Apparently the management team of the Card has lost sight of their mission.

Personal ambition for some and status quo for others had taken the place of the ship's purpose and was consuming the organization's resources toward those selfish ends. With that said and understood, the chief executive must identify with the team. When the team loses, the chief executive loses. The Head Coach is in charge of the operation, and responsible for the organization's mission. The coach's most significant objective is to prepare the team for achievement, and creating an environment for individual achievement. Effective coaches are those who are known as developers of people to be the best they can be, even if it means developing them to the point that they are able to market their skills somewhere else.

The CEO selects people who want do the job _for_ the team, **not** with the team. He wants players, not superstars. Coach Paul "Bear" Bryant, the legendary football coach of the University of Alabama, once suspended Joe Namath, his star quarterback because Joe broke the rules, he, thought he was a superstar, and above the law.

He and the other players had to know the boss would not allow anyone, not even his best player, to go against the established order.

Effective coaches surround themselves with people who have self esteem, self reliance and who can contribute to the team and the mission. If you surround yourself with third rate people, you will be the center of attention, and the others will follow with blind obedience, but you will have a third rate organization. If you surround yourself with first class people, they will express themselves, and take it upon themselves to be part of the strategic and operational planning.

You will have to hustle to keep up with them, but you will have a first rate organization. The competence and the confidence of the individual players will make or break you.

It has been my experience, that most organizations are operated by lower level executives and middle administration personnel who are mediocre at best. It's just the nature of any organization. In most organizations the real progress is made by a handful of people, the real gemstones of the enterprise. When someone with genuine gifts is identified, the responsible senior manager does not let them get lost or crushed by organizational anomalies or clever, insidious ner-do-well's.

Quoting Coach Bryant "I don't want players that are as good as anyone else; I want players who want to be better than everyone else. I want solid players, dedicated to the mission and the team, and those who strive to meet the boss' objectives, play by his rules, and believe in my plan" *(nuthin' But a Winner 1982.)*

According to Captain Mills 'orders, the mission of USS Card is: to maintain a combat ready U.S. Naval warship with a highly trained crew, that is prepared to move and function on a moment's notice to engage the enemy and prevail. The company's top management does not expect its personnel to get ready, to get prepared to meet the fiscal year's objectives. They expect them to be ready, to be prepared. When the daily routine is "fighting fires" and wrestling with poor customer service and poor production control, you know the organization's crew is not prepared to take care of business.

One may ask who is responsible for the ship's current state and its reputation. The answer of course is *management*. Subordinates assume the attitudes of their leaders. Leaders set the example for performance and behavior. The poor reputation of the ship has contributed to the demoralization of the crew. The organization's Managers must be personally concerned with the needs of the organization and have a strong sense of purpose.

Management Axioms

- Commitment to excellence in work is necessary. Everyone must be worth more than they are paid.

- Each department head has the responsibility to maintain an effective operation, directed toward the accomplishment of the organization's purpose. Anything that does not support that is extraneous.

- Managers are the stewards of the organization's resources, the natural custodians of its future, its methods, its stability and its reputation. The chief executive is the chief steward.

- When managers lose sight of the mission and fail to hold themselves or others to a level of excellence, subordinates stay in a constant state of frustration, complacency sets in and there is a general feeling that activities do not constitute any worthwhile task.

- When a manger stops producing results, you can bet that manager has lost sight of the mission.

Organizational Vision, Value, Culture and Tradition

The senior manager's *vision* for the organization follows closely on the heels of Mission. The senior manager's vision informs those in the organization, as well as those outside, how top management wants the organization to be identified now and in the future. The senior manager issues a vision statement to that effect and expects it to be the guiding light for all activities. Who you claim to be and what you are striving for is the standard that we train to and maintain on a daily basis. One Vision statement I found particularly interesting was this one from an organizational development firm. *Earn and hold the reputation for providing the most effective and respected organizational development center in our service area.*

The vision has two very significant elements; first, it is the pre-requisite for morale. The second element is no less important than the first; is the ideal position or direction in which top management would like to move the organization with regard to commitment to the continued growth and profitability of the enterprise, employee commitment to the operation and the operation's commitment to its employees.

With the organization's mission and vision are the *values* he/she established for the organization. Values are the expressed behaviors, moral obligations, performances and customs deemed as important or having an element of worth by members of the organization. A value statement reflects what management values in the enterprise. It could focus on customer satisfaction, innovation, cost effectiveness or professional competence. Whatever the expressed values, the organization will soon determine the real values by the way management rewards and punishes certain behaviors. A value statement could be stated this way; *this organization considers its reputation as the stabilizing force for its ability to carry out its mission and for its continuation in the market place.*

It is a great place to work in the minds of its employees, a responsible entity in the minds of its suppliers, a dependable, comfortable supplier in the minds of its customers, and a respectable corporate citizen in the minds of community residents.

Culture is another facet of organizational direction. Organizational culture is a possession of shared commonly held prevailing patterns of thought and behavior a fairly stable set of taken-for-granted assumptions, shared meanings, values, beliefs, perceptions, norms, and artifacts.

Culture includes sentiments that form a kind of backdrop for action. Culture also includes jargon, slang, humor, jokes and other such items and issues that attach individuals to the organization and those in it.

Among the most important elements of culture are the beliefs of employees that they can trust management to act fairly and competently. This is where vision and values mesh with the real world.

Culture explains why and how employees actually treat each other, how they treat customers, how they treat equipment, how they treat management, the level of respect for their job and how in turn, management treats these items. How they treat each other is in direct portion to how they think the organization as an entity values them. This is demonstrated by what the management team displays as important. If it is not those essential elements that pertain to organizational achievement from individual performance it is readily noticed and punished.

How employees treat each other is directly affected by **worthwhile work**. The very subjects that create an environment of success will, if not maintained, create an environment of demoralization. All personnel must know that what they are doing is necessary to the well being of the organization. To keep your people coming back for more every day, in bad weather and good, under high activity or low, the organization's managers must provide an environment that produces professional and personal fulfillment *most* of the time. Being needed, knowing that one is doing something useful and necessary, and can do it well, is an essential ingredient of human happiness. Work done well and to the best of one's ability is one of the most satisfying of human experiences. The crew must have something worthwhile to do each day that will lead them toward some measurable objective.

The most noteworthy failure of the Card's management team was the provision of worthwhile work with measurable outcomes. There is no commitment from management or the crew. The ship is in poor mechanical condition. Housekeeping, maintenance and safety are not given adequate attention, and the crew is poorly trained. Safety, housekeeping, maintenance and training are critical, but nothing is more important that performing a worthwhile task and seeing results from your effort. *The common denominator for success is worthwhile work. Without work, one loses vision, confidence and the determination to succeed.*

The most demoralizing aspect of work-life is the realization that one's work unit is incapable of achieving expected results.

People spend more than a third of their lives in the workplace; it should be enjoyable most of the time. General Dwight D. Eisenhower once said, *"Only the man that is happy in his work can be happy in his home and with his friends. Happiness in work means the performer must know it to be worthwhile work, suited to his temperament, his age, experience, natural abilities and capacity for performance of a higher order."*

In the list of necessary provisions for a functional organizational culture are; competent management and leadership, provision for the elements of a stable work environment such as policies and procedures that guide the organization's society and culture and an environment for achievement that includes; training and skill competency development.

Recognition and rewards are right up there with the other essential items. Let's not forget an appropriate wage that is in line with the industry and the community. Management must make an investment in equipment. Frustration experienced by high tech professionals, forced to use obsolete equipment, will result in dissatisfaction and loss of commitment. When high talent is not being used, people with marketable skills who are not challenged will go elsewhere.

Tradition plays a significant role in organizational culture and the behavior that results from the daily application of that culture. Organizational traditions have a critical impact on those who are employed by it. When employees accept the traditions as an important identifier of the value of the organization, and those traditions are constantly spotlighted by top management, they try to live up those traditions. Many *old line* industries, universities and social organizations are steeped in honored traditions that set them apart as unique among others. Those who identify with those traditions pride themselves in maintaining the traditions and discipline their behavior to conform to the expectations that embody the traditions.

Training greatly affects culture. Training embeds a respect for culture and tradition as it develops those performance patterns and predictable behavior so relevant to the maintenance of the culture. Training promotes discipline, self control and an approach to the job that is consistent with tradition. Training in organizational culture begins with the orientation program and continues through on the job competence development. Training affects self image and perceptions of expected behavior are factors that influence changes in culture. The expectations of individuals define for them what they should do under various circumstances in their particular job, and how they think others, superiors, peers, and subordinates should also behave in relation to their positions. Training produces competence and with competence comes feelings of worthwhile-ness, which is an important factor in morale. We will deal with morale and training, in more detail later.

We explored the impact that vision and value has on an organization and how they set the tone for the culture, and the in the organization's make up. Culture and tradition are two other aspects that identify the organization. People come and go but the culture remains.

In some cases the culture will change over time, depending on how it is influenced by management through rewards and punishments of individual and collective behaviors. It is imperative that subordinates understand and share the expectations of senior management, specifically those of the chief executive, and can share the goals, values, vision, objectives and expectations that person brings to the organization.

But make no mistake about the significance of management's respect for these stated elements of the organization's culture. I was called in to a major manufacturer of institutional casework to do a management training needs analysis. The company's executives were under the impression that first line supervisors were not treating their subordinates properly. The new chief executive officer felt very strongly about managing the organization's culture with published mission, value and vision statements.

He instituted a company-wide program to indoctrinate all employees on his vision for the organization, his values for how the company's managers and employees were to take seriously, and the mission of the organization stated in clear succinct fashion. He had these statements framed and were hung on almost every flat surface in the building (not too much of an overstatement) He issued laminated cards to all employees, and had framed copies for every desk in the organization.

The statements were based on appropriate consideration for customers, suppliers, employees and the public at large. It spoke of excellent treatment and respect for every entity involved in its operation as being critical to its success. The published statements spoke of the rich tradition of elegance and excellence that the hallmark of the organization success and reputation. What I discovered was that no one in management took these pronouncements seriously. The chief executive was certain that everyone, especially his executive team lived by these creeds. But blatant short circuits in quality control, circumventing customer service and substituting specified items with less expensive ones, soon showed the hourly employees that management was blowing smoke. Employees were suppose to be part of a "better place to work" society, but were not called on to offer suggestions, and poor treatment not the least of which were discrepancies in their profit sharing soon brought a counter-productive attitude in the hourly ranks.

The president called an emergency meeting with the entire management staff from executive vice president to first line supervisor. He read them the riot act and established a reporting system to ensure the mission, vision and value pronouncements would be a living way of life in this organization. He set up employee teams to proved guidance for implementing and sustaining the program, particularly those relating to customer service and employee involvement.

He required all human resources to introduce the mission, vision and value statements to all new employees during the orientation process. They had to write a statement as to what they meant and how they will respect them during their time with the company. He also required all employees to retake the complete new orientation program on or near their anniversary date during their performance evaluation time.

They had to write a paper stating what their department did over the past year to enforce those three doctrines.

As we have seen on the *U.S.S. Card,* as in any other organization, culture is not constant. Values and norms change as events affect the population involved. These shifts in values may precede or accompany political shifts, such as a significant change at the senior management level, as they will bring in their own values and visions, or a major change in the status or position of an organization in the market place.

The officers and crew of the *Card* did not realize they were experiencing turbulent times. They did not realize the organization's culture had devolved to what Clayton Christiansen and Thomas Davenport *(Harvard Business Review)* calls accidental culture. Accidental Culture, they say, is caused by the inaction or incorrect actions consequential to poor decisions by the organization's leaders.

While they were dissatisfied with the way things were the officers and crew were comfortable with the existing culture, which made very few demands on them, dissuading them from examining their status which would indicate a need for change.

The *USS Card's* organizational culture did not change with Captain Gallagher it began before he took command. It began to change when the conditions required them to miss week end drills at sea and the annual combat readiness exercise.

Training took a big hit also since they were not able to do simulations in underway conditions with any semblance of fidelity. The *Card's* organizational structure was adjusted to accommodate its pier-bound condition when certain officer billets and enlisted billets were discontinued. Organizational structure greatly influences the culture because behavior is not random and is directed by some degree of formalization toward a goal, and the decisions made concerning structure contributed to the change in culture. Captain Gallagher's decision to allow Mr. Winthrop to exercise his discretion with regard to the Card's condition, and Lieutenant Commander McCormick's acquiescence simply contributed to the change in culture. The culture deteriorated into lethargy after a while, and the executive team contributed to its downward spiral by not holding itself and the crew to proper naval discipline and competence.

Captain Mills recognized the importance of changing the culture on the *Card*. It is the current culture that is hampering effective operations. Changing norms, roles and values that are deeply entrenched in an organizational culture is a difficult and in many cases impossible venture. Captain Mills must bring the entity, and the ship's company back to the traditions and norms it enjoyed before it was allowed to deteriorate. Captain Mills began that process at his first visit when he changed the uniform of the quarterdeck watch.

He required the ship's company to wear clean pressed uniforms, with shirt tails tucked in and proper rank displayed.

He required officers to come to dinner in a dress uniform. He imposed his values on the organization's culture when he required the ship's officers to submit standard, traditional reports.

He emphasized the importance of training. He ordered a thorough clean up and paint job, He ordered all department heads to develop and implement plans for complying with naval regulations and standards.

He took action to get the *Card* and its crew out to sea and actually do the jobs they were expected to perform, and to once again fulfill a useful function.

For the *Card,* or any other organization to be effective, to grow, or to survive at all, it must fulfill some useful function. The common goals set by the founders of the organization must result in some product or service which is useful, and holds a certain sense of pride to those in the organization and is desired by others outside the organization.

Captain Mills' first objective toward changing the culture that will lead to accomplishing the mission on board the *Card* is evident. He must get underway. He must get production out. He must direct their attention to the task at hand. A lethargic organization does not usually realize the condition they are in until they are called on to produce to a higher standard. When the crew attempts to get the ship underway they will discover the deplorable state they are in. Only then can the captain begin to make corrections that will bring them to combat readiness. The crew on the *Card* may need to experience failure, before than can begin to move toward success.

Management Axioms:

- The common denominator for success is worthwhile work. Without work one loses vision, confidence and the determination to succeed.

- The senior executive and the senior executive staff's vision and value objectives set the tone for the culture, and behavior in the organization. It is imperative that subordinates understand and share the expectations of senior management, specifically those of the chief executive, and can share the goals, values, vision, objectives and expectations that person brings to the organization

The Turnaround Project

After considering the Card's current state captain Mills decided that to bring it to combat ready status called for a project management approach. A project is a one-time set of activities that ends with a specific accomplishment. A set of non routine tasks performed in a certain sequence leading to a specific goal with a distinct start and finish date, a limited set of resources. Some resources may need to be borrowed or contracted for.

The project objective was clearly spelled out in Captain Mill's orders "Bring the ship and its crew up to combat readiness and join the squadron for combat readiness exercises in GTMO in six months."

To take on any project, especially one with this level of difficulty requires some critical assessments. The senior management team or board of directors has to agree that the outcome is necessary enough to approve the project and that the organization is worth the effort and the expenditures needed to produce the effort. The power brokers must have faith in the project manager, especially if the project has a limited expectation of success or there are other risk factors. Not just the senior executives, but the project manager must make some critical assessments:

1. Assess the risk to his/her career and to the organization. If the project fails is the payoff worth the investment?

2. Assess the project manager's management skills: Does the project manager have the management skills to pull the organization together and direct the available energies and resources to that end?

3. Assess money set aside for the budget is it sufficient to secure the needed resources?

4. Assess the management team's knowledge, skills and abilities match them with those required to implement the project's plans. Do they have the talent, aptitude, the temperament and the desire to make it happen or can they be brought up to the task?

5. Assess the skills of the technical crew. Do they have the talent, the temperament and the desire to make it happen or can they be brought up to the task?

6. Assess the charter. Is it clear as to what the project entails, the costs and the risks and the conditions under which the project will be carried out? It must also include the project manager's access to the project's sponsors. Surely the captain did not go blindly into this project. ComResDesRon, like any board of directors or senior management team, would have required a written plan and they would have approved the plan. The project manager and the power brokers (senior executives or board of directors) agree on the outcome and the expected completion date. The project manager's plan includes:

- A plan to meet requirements with defined interface responsibilities between the work units and time lines and progress measurements.

- A plan for staffing the project with qualified personnel and establish performance measurements for evaluating their effectiveness and application of talent and skills.

- A plan for developing the project team for effectively interfacing with each other to carry out the plan

- A budget and methods for securing the funding.

- Time lines and control systems for managing the continuous daily operations to ensure project is on schedule and budget.

- A system for keeping the senior power brokers informed of status progress against plan objectives and time lines.

There are some "Gotchas" and concerns to avoid when a new project begins that can spell disaster which include, but are not limited to:

- Lack of experience with this type of project.

- Underestimating the technical difficulty

- Making overly optimistic assumptions about the outcomes and completion dates.

- Getting too involved with details or the technical, rather than the management aspects of the project.

- Ignoring "gut feeling" concerns or not searching for concerns, or doubts, and then not addressing them promptly head on.

- Failure to secure team ownership of the project. Ownership is arguably the most important factor in securing the expected outcomes within the allocated time frame and budget.

The concurrent projects

Other projects needing to be in place and making steady progress simultaneously:

1. Changing the ship's company's perception of themselves, and their ship from "Carp" to "*Card*", from old bucket to a magnificent vessel, from part time or week end sailors to competent professional maritime seaman.

2. Ship clean up and paint project to un-clutter the work place in order to allow for easy movement and psychological well-being. To show the crew the Navy is willing to invest in the comfort of the workplace. This includes repairing and beautifying the ambiance that is unique to the maritime service.

3. Repair, retrofit and upgrade all operating equipment in order to get the ship underway and fully functional.

4. Upgrade the crew's maritime and combat assignments in order to meet ComResDesRon objectives.

Assembling a project team:

The *Card's* executive team is not a team. We can assume that Robert Mills, or ComResDesRon or both have determined they have the talent for accomplishing the mission and with some guiding and coaching from the captain, they can eventually succeed. For a project team or any management team to be effective there are certain criteria that must be evident: there must be commitment to the common course, standards, goals and specific outcomes.

There must be, agreement on expectations of the team and the interfacing of team individuals and active open communication with free and helpful exchange of information

Project team development usually involves a four step process:

1. Forming – coming together to learn of the project and their place in it.

2. Storming – getting used to working together and working for the project manager. There will usually be some disconnect and miscommunications and maybe even some jealousy and turf protecting. Re-defining goals and refocusing direction is inevitable.

3. Norming – cohesion begins to develop, and respect for the others and the project begins to gel. Some successes are reported and the recognition of achievement because of the others is within reach.

4. Performing - the individual contributions are working, interfacing is fluid and project objectives are being met. The planned outcome is inevitable.

Chapter 2

**Storm Warnings
Friday, 13 February 1970
Reserve Drill Week End
USS Card - Pier Side
US Coast Guard Base, Curtis Bay Maryland**

1400: The drill weekend began on **Friday, 13 February. T**here were a large number of the reserve-enlisted crewmen absent. After consulting with the officers, Captain Mills decided enough of the critically skilled members were present that they could get underway safely.

For three hours the engineers worked to light off the engines and boilers, but they could not get them to stay on long enough to sustain adequate pressure even for a preliminary checkout.

The other departments sensed the frustration taking place in Engineering, and their efforts were desultory. By the end of the drill weekend only 40% of the reserve ship's company was present.

When the standards of discipline are no longer important and no one is concerned with maintaining standards and they become absurd, the breath goes out of the operation. When there is no morale there is no motivation or desire to engage the emotional energy necessary to make a contribution. Discipline is the foundation for productivity. Discipline represents the ultimate product of good leadership in developing group solidarity, esprit, motivation and skillful performance. It is the individual or group attitude that insures prompt obedience to orders and initiation of appropriate actions in the absence of orders.

**Saturday, 14 February 1970
USS Card Pier side
US Coast Guard Yard Curtis Bay, Maryland**

0900: The customary Change of Command Ceremony took place as scheduled on 14 February at zero nine hundred (9:00AM). The ship was too small for all the guests to stand on the *Card's* weather decks so chairs were set up on the pier. Sailors stood in sharp dress blue uniforms, spit shined shoes and pea-coats. They were at parade rest in division formation all along the weather decks. Invited guests took their places in the chairs on the pier and dignitaries were seated in chairs on the fantail facing aft. A podium was set up near the gaff for the two commanding officers to exchange positions.

Commander Mills saluted the acting Captain, and said, "Pursuant to Command Order 2215 I relieve you as Commanding Officer of the *USS. Card.*"

Lieutenant Commander McCormick returned the salute and said, "I stand relieved." He then saluted the new Captain and the new Captain returned the salute.

[Footnote: anyone who is assigned command of a ship is referred to as "Captain," even though their actual rank may be less. In this case, Robert Mills' rank -- his pay grade -- is one level less than a Navy Captain's].

Captain Mills then addressed the crew: "All standing orders will remain in effect until further notice. There will be no major changes made until I have had a chance to evaluate our situation. I don't believe in removing fences until I have determined why they were put there in the first place. In the next several weeks, I will be touring the ship's spaces. I will be meeting with the ship's officers and crew. I want to get to know each of you and I want you to get to know me."

He paused and turned his eyes toward his officer corps then back to his crew.

"I think you'll find my philosophy and style of management will be easy to work with. I believe in competence, development, and in holding each person responsible for applying that competence. Each of you will be given an opportunity to make a substantial contribution to this ship. We will have an active, fully operational facility during my administration. Make no mistake we will join the squadron for combat exercises in Guantanamo Bay in July. We will begin preparing for that event at our next drill."

He turned to LCDR McCormick, and directed him to dismiss the crew. The Executive Officer turned to the Command Chief Petty Officer and said. "Command Chief, dismiss the crew."

The Command Chief saluted the Lieutenant Commander, who returned his salute. He turned toward the crew and shouted; "Crew dismissed."

Mister Winthrop stood to the microphone and announced, "That concludes the Change of Command Ceremony, Ladies and Gentlemen. Thank you all for attending."

The guests stood and went their way. The senior officers and the dignitaries were announced as they left the ship preceded by the ringing of the ship's bell as before. Everyone noticed when Commander Mills stepped onto the brow, saluted the Quarterdeck Officer then turned to salute the Ensign, the Boatswain's mate rang the bell four times, Ding-Ding, Ding-Ding, and announced "*USS Card* Departing." It was now official: he was *USS Card's* Commanding Officer.

The new Captain's first meeting with the *Card's* officers began promptly at fifteen hundred (3:00 PM). They took their seats around the wardroom table in their assigned seats according to rank.

The wardroom is a general-purpose room that serves as the officers' dining area, a formal meeting room, and the officers' lounge. The main feature of the wardroom is a long table surrounded on the long sides by dinning style leather cushioned chairs, five on the starboard side, and five on the portside.

At the other end of the table, aft, was the "official" head of the table where prominently sat the Captain's dinning chair.

It was different from the other chairs. The most significant item was the word "Captain" embroidered in the cordovan colored leather. Behind the Captain's chair was the door that led to the passage way out of "officer's country."

The table was covered with a white linen cloth with the ship's seal embroidered in the center.

At the end of the wardroom, forward, was a counter where fresh hot coffee, cold drinks and snacks were always present. Behind the counter was a kitchen where the officer's stewards prepared their meals and snacks.

Along the port bulkhead were leather covered wing back chairs each with its own table and reading lamp. Along the starboard bulkhead was a book case, filled with books that extended the entire length of the wardroom about waist high. The top of the book case was reserved for the officers to place their hats when they enter the wardroom. The hats are arranged in rank and time-in-grade order beginning with the Captain's hat nearest the Captain's position at the wardroom table.

The Captain took his place at the head of the table and the meeting began. The stewards had placed a coffee cup and saucer in front of each position. The cups bore the ship's insignia. The stewards had also placed a leather binder, with the ships insignia, at each position. The officers sat in rank and time-in-grade order, beginning with the Captain at the head of the table, Lieutenant Commander McCormick, the XO, on his right and Mr. Winthrop the Officer in Charge (Operations Officer and Navigator) on his left.

The ship's Executive Officer is usually the "mess president." The Commanding Officer normally dines alone and is not a member of the wardroom, but is invited to join the members for special occasions. On a ship the size of the CARD the Captain often dines in the wardroom and holds meetings there.

The ship's new Captain addressed the *Card's* officer corps: "Ladies and Gentlemen, as the new Commanding Officer of *USS Card* I have been entrusted with the welfare of this ship and of its crew. I intend to fulfill my responsibilities and to do so in an exemplary manner. You, having prior experience on board, will help me carry out this mission. You heard my message to the ship's company. I stressed competence, development, and responsibility. Nowhere is this more important than in the wardroom. I expect professionalism from every one of you." He paused to ensure full attention."

The officers were stoic. All eyes were focused on this management consultant the Navy brass chose to captain their ship.

"For the next two weeks, I will be orienting myself to the *Card*. That should give me enough time to get a good feel for the ship's routine and for areas in which I want to make changes. If you find me in your department's spaces, I'm just familiarizing myself. I will have many questions which, I trust, you ladies and gentlemen will be able to answer. If you do not know the answers, then don't act like you do. You should know first off to keep me informed and to give me correct and complete information.

I am much more forgiving of bad news if I receive it in time to do something about it, or at least before I hear it from ComResDesRon." He leaned forward, his elbows on the table, his hands clasp together near his chin. He breathed in.

"I am looking forward to working with you. I realize a change in command is a stressful ordeal, but now that it is behind us we can concentrate on running this ship. Are there any questions?" The Captain looked around the wardroom into nine silent faces.

"Well, if there are no questions, I have a few requests. Mr. Winthrop, you and Mr. McCormick will have a meeting every Thursday. There will be plenty to talk about. One item I want to see is the daily eight O'clock reports. Please ensure that all required items are included. I want to be kept fully informed of the ship's status." *(8:00 AM reports in port 8:00 PM reports at sea)*

Lieutenant Winthrop spoke up, "Excuse me Sir, but Captain Gallagher didn't require us to include a daily draft report. The readings on the pier side of the ship have been painted over and taking the readings from the other side requires sending someone down in a boatswain's chair. With all the required safety precautions, it's too much time and effort out of the men's day for such a routine item." He paused to see how the skipper would react to this information. The Captain said nothing.

"Also, the daily muster isn't included in the eight o'clock report. The Command Duty Officer takes care of it."

Lieutenant Winthrop," the Captain replied evenly, "I suggest you have the draft readings repainted before our Thursday meeting, and from now on include the daily muster in the eight o'clock report. You will conduct a zero eight hundred report and a twenty hundred report until further notice."

The Captain paused to see if Lieutenant Winthrop had any further comments, then continued, "Another report I want, in the proper format and timely fashion, is the weekly preventive maintenance report. We all know how important proper maintenance is, especially on a ship this old. When the PMS (Preventative Maintenance Schedules) inspectors come on board in April, I expect to show them a 100% completion rate on required maintenance. Commander McCormick," he said, addressing the Executive Officer who sat at his right, "What is our current PMS completion rate?"

"I don't have that information right now, Sir. It will take me some time to put that together."

"Please do so," he said adamantly. "Once that information is together, we must have a plan and work systematically toward fulfilling it."

This time it was Lieutenant Fridel who spoke up. "Captain, there's no way we can make 100%. Many of the tools required for the checks aren't even on board and we don't have the money to buy them."

"What happened to the tools?" asked Captain Mills.

Lieutenant Fridel shrugged, "They've disappeared over the years, Sir."

Captain Mills considered the Lieutenant's answer and then said, "Bring me the requisitions for the required tools. I'll get them ordered, even if I have to deal directly with the Squadron Supply Officer. Until then, borrow tools from the other ships, if you can."

"In addition, Mister Fridel, since most of the major repair work on this ship will concern the Engineering Department you will be responsible for giving me a daily ship-wide work-in-progress report."

Looking around the wardroom, he added, "Other department heads, keep Mister Fridel updated as to your requirements and progress so he can submit complete reports. Mister Hooper, as First Lieutenant I will expect a separate report from you. You will conduct an inspection and make a list of items that need work that is not normally part of the official list required by Bu-Ships (Bureau of Ships)."

He turned to face the Weapons Officer. "Lieutenant Grubaugh, I need to be informed of which systems will be used during the exercises in GITMO. Also, a list of the ammunition we will need to take on."

He turned toward his XO. "By the way, Mr. McCormick, When is our gunnery crew scheduled for the exercise qualification school at Little Creek?"

"I can't remember offhand, Captain," said the Exec, "I'll have to check my files."

"Do we have a scheduled time, Mister McCormick?"

"I don't think so, sir, but I will check into it."

"Please do so," again there was no weakness in the word please. "then, drop by my cabin this evening with the information." Again the Captain paused before continuing, "Mister Goldsmith, I need a copy of the ship's manning document with rank and time-in-grade information. And I want to see the Personnel Records files on the ship's officers and senior enlisted E-6, E-7 and E-8."

"Petty Officer Williams can get that for you Captain, he is my Yeoman."

"Very well. One more thing; the uniform of the day for quarter deck watches and Officers of the Day will be dress blues, until April when we shift to whites then it will be dress whites." I noticed some sloppy uniforms. I want all of the ship's company to wear a clean pressed uniform every day, with shirts tucked in and their correct rank appropriately displayed. If we are to be professional, we need to look professional."

The Captain lifted his yellow pad, glanced at it and sat it down in front of him. He lifted his eyes toward his officers. "I want the drill weekends to be just that, drill weekends. I want each department to conduct several drills each day. I want every action that will be encountered in a combat situation practiced, over and over again until it becomes second nature."

The officers looked at each other. Each had a look of dread on their faces. This was something they had not done, and were not very confident in their ability to carry out this order.

The Captain made a note on the yellow pad in front of him. Thinking his attention was focused on the notes he was making, the officers looked at each other with expressions of trepidation. This was a ploy Mills used quite often when investigating problems on other ships. He was quite aware of the anxiety he was producing among the officers, and that was exactly what he was doing. Still looking at the words he had written, he said, "Much of the information I requested is not available." He looked up, his eyes scanning the officer corps.

He paused a moment. "a clear indication that something is dreadfully wrong. Reports measure not only current status, but serve as an effective control method as it shows progress toward meeting objectives. When an activity is measured, it is tantamount to getting it accomplished. Reports keep the organization on track. If a manager is not able to provide an instant report on the health and welfare of their department, they are not on top of things."

His focus, once again, went to the pad. As he scribbled on the pad he spoke in a tone similar to a physician writing a prescription; "As soon as we are done here, I want each of you to draw up a plan for what your department is expected to do in the GITMO exercise and attach a training plan to prepare for it."

The captain turned to face the supply officer. Mr. Goldsmith I want you to order a sufficient number of the *Card's* coat of arms patches. I want them issued to all the crew, at the next drill weekend, including officers. I want them sewn on all working jackets. Give them some extras for their civilian jackets. Also arrange to have the ships coat of arms displayed on a banner to cover the bulkhead in the mess deck, and the officer's wardroom. I want it large so it can't be overlooked. I want to see our motto displayed everywhere. . . *Seek – Strike – Prevail*".

A surprise look came over the officers, some smiled others frowned.

"Aye Sir" Mr. Goldsmith responded.

"Oh I'm not through yet Mr. Goldsmith. I noticed there were no ships identification patches in the ship's store. I want you to stock pile those patches and I want ten of them issued to every enlisted person aboard."

He turned his attention to Mr. McCormick. "Mr. McCormick, order the enlisted to sew these patches on their uniforms. We will have a sea bag inspection at the April drill and I want to see those patches on every enlisted white and blue uniform."

"Aye sir."

He turned to his XO. "Lieutenant Commander McCormick, see that is changed on the plan of the day. With that we will adjourn."

The Captain stood up. The officers stood up pushing their chairs out behind them with the back of their knees. He removed his hat from its place, inserted it under his left arm and walked to the door. He turned to face his executive team. "You have your orders. I will be expecting your reports. I will meet with each of you soon.

I want you to be prepared for that meeting." He turned toward the door, twisted the door handle and it creaked open. Still holding onto the door handle, he turned again to face the officers. "You would do well to keep in mind your commission as officers of the *Card.* Your commission is to maintain a combat ready U.S. Naval **warship** . . . with a highly trained crew, prepared to move and function at a moment's notice . . . to engage the enemy . . . and prevail."

His expression was one of resolve. The officers could feel it. He placed his cap on his head, turned and walked through the door and pulled it closed behind him. The officers looked at each other with expressions of trepidation. They all knew this guy was not going to be easy to work with.

It was eleven fifteen when the captain exited the wardroom. As he pulled the door closed the loudspeaker over his head came to life, and a strong male voice announced: "Now sweepers, sweepers man your brooms let's have a clean sweep down fore and aft. Clean all lower decks, ladders and passageways, empty all trash cans. Now sweepers." There was a slight pause then the voice came on again; "Knock off ship's work and prepare for the noon meal."

"Business as usual aboard a US Navy ship," thought Mills.

Captain Mills found Yeoman Petty Officer First Class Otis Williams in the Administrative office. As he entered the office he noticed the gold eagle with three gold chevrons sewed on the left upper arm of his uniform and three gold hash marks on the left forearm indicating at least 12 years of exemplary service. He had the word on this man. He was handpicked by Sorenson himself. He came on board with Captain Gallagher. Williams was one of those guys with a special set of skills. He knew everyone on the ship. Apparently he knew everyone in the Navy who can make anything happen, or knows someone who knows someone. He was one of those rare individuals one wants to get to know because he can get things done. The more people who get in his rolodex, the more effective he becomes. How he keeps up with all his contacts is a mystery. There have been times when he had multiple projects going just to get one item he needed.

The Yeoman stood up quickly when the Captain entered the administration office. The Captain noticed the Yeoman already had the files he would be requesting on his desk in rank order.

"As you were Yeoman Williams."

"Thank you Sir." The Yeoman sat down in the chair behind the desk.

 "I see you already have the officer's service jackets ready. I appreciate your proactive consideration."

"I have been in a change of command situation before Captain. I know you have been briefed on each of the officers, but I presumed you wanted to see the "official" files and fitness reports. I also retrieved the files of all E-6, E-7s and E8's In case you wanted to see them as well."

"You presumed correctly Yeoman Williams."

Williams placed his hand on another stack of personnel files and pushed them toward the Captain. "Sir, may I suggest you take special notice of Chief Gruber's file and mine. You may also be interested in seeing Radioman First Class Anderson's records, and Radarman Second Class Henson. We have a weathered Boatswain's Mate on the reserve roster that is also a person of interest, Ezra Furman."

"Very well, Williams, I will trust your judgment."

Williams smiled, and placed three fingers on a radio message, which had been lying face down on the desk, and slid it toward the Captain. "I have a friend at NavBase, who has a friend at BUPERS (pronounced Bu-Pers – Bureau of Personnel) who thinks this may be of interest to you as well."

The Captain retrieved the paper and read it. "Jawarski huh?"

"I played poker with him in GITMO. He was on the adversary team and knows what they look for during the exercises. We can get him......If.....you want...."

"Well now Yeoman Williams, it appears as though you may be someone I need to keep an eye on."

"Well an ear anyway...Captain."

They smiled at each other and nodded. Both men had been around long enough to recognize a worthy ally. Captain Mills placed the stack of folders in his leather bag and exited the room. He entered his cabin on the 0-3 level across from Radio Central. It was eleven fifty five.

"Mess call, clear the mess decks," came the word over the 1-MC.

Assessment Chapter 2
Storm Warnings

Attitudes, Job Satisfaction, Compliance and Cooperation

The forming segment of the captain's project team doesn't seem to be coming together. We should not be surprised; the wardroom (executive leadership) has not been a team for quite some time. He has stated and restated the project's expected outcome, but so far no one has taken it seriously. By the defensive stance taken by the officers in the first meeting with captain Mills, it appears that they were more concerned about their careers than the state of the organization. We can see they were bent on carrying out their own agenda at the expense of the organization. But they also knew they have not been producing, and are now in a mental state stagnated by doubt, congealed by fear and demoralized by defeat. To them, the only safe environment was status quo. The senior manager must help them deal with this attitude. Any behavior on the part of management that suggests a preference for the status quo will breed mediocrity into organizational policies and penalize individuals who rock the boat by demonstrating initiative.

Initiative exposes those who are steeped in mediocrity and organizational exposure leads to punishment to the one who does the exposing and rewarding those who continue in the quest for status quo. Whether intentional or not these messages tend to show rewards for continued mediocrity and punishment for any show of initiative. Human behavior punishes behavior we do not want continued, and rewards behavior we do want continued. Punishment is any action that discourages a behavior, and reward is any action that encourages a behavior. More often than not managers are not aware of their rewarding and punishing behavior. These negative attitudes must be corrected. Attitudes are expressed by behavior. The effective manager must insist on a change of behavior first then attitudes will follow.

As shocking as it appears to the newly appointed executive there are those subordinate managers who seem to defy or challenge the new boss. When an entire organization falls into lethargy they do not recognize their condition until someone reveals it. At first it would seem that they thought the Captain's plans were unrealistic and would fail. Perhaps they did realize the condition of the ship and that their own careers were stagnant. Most likely they were afraid he would succeed and expose their complacency. Deep down inside they had lost faith in themselves, because they had not scored any successes in a long time. Whatever their reasons they were not justifiable and their resistance to the captain's presence stemmed from the discomfort of a realistic assessment of the facts.

The senior manager has a responsibility to subordinate managers who are not producing. The senior manager does not grant pity or inflict malice.

Help them to recommit to their mission, help them to get a plan for satisfying that mission. Tell them from this point on they will be held accountable for applying themselves to the accomplishment of their objectives.

After all ComResDesRon is not interested in ruining careers; they realize a leadership problem exists. They want the crew trained, and the ship made ready for the GTMO exercise.

The Captain said there is a bad attitude on this ship. Job performance, job behavior and military bearing of the officers and the crew are unacceptable. It is easy to understand why. There is no commitment to discipline, no commitment to the mission, no commitment to the organization, and the only cooperation between departments is to maintain the status quo. There is no real job involvement.

It seems the officers had convinced themselves that no one realized they were not producing. ComResDesRon told the captain he would bring the ship up to combat readiness. It was obvious they had not been to sea for drill weekends or participated in squadron exercises. ComResDesRon had apparently not insisted on production. It may be ComResDesRon expected Captain Gallagher to renew the organization but either he could not or he thought, as so many others did, that it was not worth saving.

Captain Gallagher was removed even though it would be three months before Commander Mills would be available to take on the operation. This is classic example of the old management axiom; *it is better to leave a position vacant than to give it to someone who can't handle it.* This is true even in the senior ranks, or maybe especially in the senior ranks. ComResDesRon made the commitment to saving the ship because it could have value again. The ship's company and the ship's officers must be a part of the plan and share in its renewal and up to now there was no one in the command role who could secure that participation.

The officers and crew had slipped into a state of mediocrity but don't take it for granted that the marginal employee is second rate because it is their nature. There are sour grapes in every basket, but fewer than you might imagine. The executive must make a determined effort to draw the best from their people. Keep them informed as to how the organization is progressing and how their contributions are influencing that progress. Bend over backwards to spark their job interest before writing them off.

Get them involved in decisions and plans, not merely routine chores. Success flourishes in an atmosphere of success, not failure! Motivation to accomplish results tends to increase when people have meaningful goals toward which to work.

Rarely have I seen an organization as demoralized as this one. I have seen entire departments in this condition but only twice in my career have I walked into a situation such as this. One was a closely held company that allowed no outside management influence, the other was a family owned business that operated for the benefit of the family members, and like the closely held company it allowed no outside management influence. Poor leadership and management, poor training and lack of accountability has changed the focus from highly trained combat readiness prepared to move at a moment's notice, engage the enemy and prevail, to protection of our delusion at all cost.

Losing sight of the vision has caused them to lose confidence in themselves as individuals, in themselves as a team, in their leadership and in their organization.

The natural progression of confidence loss is loss of security, which is manifested in discouragement and defensiveness. But regardless of where they are in this pit, there is a way out.

Captain Mills began by giving them an important assignment. In this case the captain needed to get his subordinate officers involved with the recovery operation. His first tactic was to change the mindset of the ship's company and it was one that required very little professional competence. He changed their look by insisting on dress uniform for the quarter deck watches and the evening meal. He ordered the ship's company to wear clean pressed uniforms of the day with shirts tucked in and appropriate rank displayed. To establish identity he issued orders for the ships logo patch, with its motto to be provided for all the crew, and required them to wear it. It displayed it in the mess decks and in the officer's wardroom to assist in focusing their attention on the organization and what it stood for and can again. He wanted the motto; *seek – strike - prevail* to encourage them to be the organization that is prepared to meet the motto's challenge. To further ingrain identity he required them to wear the ship's identity patch on their white and blue uniforms. To make sure they did, he ordered a sea bag inspection.

The Captain had to get the crew's mind off the past and the current state of affairs and give them a vision of what can be, and the belief that they can make it happen. They need to buy into the captain's vision and actively participate in making it a reality. They need to identify with the ship, its motto and strive to bring the captain's vision to fruition. They must focus on being successful not dwelling on failure. *To dwell on failure will result in failure. To dwell on success will almost always result in success.*

The 1914 Broadway play "Pygmalion" was a modern version of the ancient Greek play by the same name. Two film versions were produced, one in 1935, the other in 1978, entitled "My fair Lady". Professor Higgins believed he could transform Liza Doolittle from a street urchin to a sophisticate lady of society. He convinced her he could do it, and then spent time and attention making it happen.

Eventually Liza believed she could do it and that was the key to the success of the experiment.

The organization's leaders must provide a clear mission, a vision and positive expectations of themselves and those whom they lead. Along with this role and mission clarity they also provided positive expectations, positive reinforcement, personal attention and extensive training.

Next the Captain began a campaign to remove clutter from the ship and from their minds. He ordered a thorough clean up fore and aft, stem to stern. He wanted everything that was not required or unusable to be discarded; He ordered a paint job for the entire ship.

It is amazing how clutter and neglect gets in the way of effective thinking, and the free flow of operational business activities.

The clean-up operation was a big deal. He wanted them to change their point of view from what they thought they were to what they could be.

Once the entire ship's company accomplished something worthwhile it was a small step to the next method of renewal. The C.O. ordered each department head to complete a department assessment and compare the status with combat exercise requirements. This activity is followed by working with the captain to develop a plan to meet those requirements.

Once the department heads realistically examine the status of their assigned areas of responsibility they will recognize its deplorable condition and allow the captain to help them take action to correct it. He told them he would visit with them and help them with their clean-up and "get-well" programs. His intention was to spend one-on-one time to encourage them, keep them from being overwhelmed with the task in front of them.

The captain called their attention to the training section of the "Get Well" plan He said "Now this next item is extremely important. Turn in your binders to the section marked *Training for GTMO*". What was that all about? Training for a future activity creates positive expectations. The crew's perception of their ship was one of failure and disappointment, one that had no expectations of ever being in the thick of battle again. That perception lead to a self fulfilling prophesy a situation that dragged them down into the dregs of failure. They had signed on to be a viable element in the nation's defense.

They signed on to participate in combat operations, and they used to look forward to the battles in the GTMO exercises.

Training for the GTMO experience would begin the process of changing the perception of failure to a perception of success. Engaging in this worthwhile task offered the promise of the GTMO experience again. This training would also lead to other changes in performance and self esteem as they once again witness the exhilaration of accomplishment and personal successes.

Lieutenant Winthrop is a unique bird, but I have seen many dilettantes like him in industry and government, and primarily in a family owned business and closely held corporations.

They have a superficial interest in a discipline; they just dabble in the field while creating turmoil for everyone else who is trying to make a difference. Because of their affiliation with those in authority their attitudes and behaviors rub off on others in the organization. They favor their position and status but at the expense of the organization, and those who, because of this condition are trapped in career dead ends. King Louis XVI recognized this condition in his own court when he said "After me, the deluge."

People will often follow a demagogue to their own destruction because he makes them feel good, and it is an easy path to follow. People, like rivers tend to take the path of least resistance.

If a manager has tried everything to get cooperation and has failed the next thing to do is require compliance. It is a small step from compliance to cooperation.

Management Axioms:

- All managers must resist the temptation to use the goose to feather their own nests.

- Discontinue reward systems that encourage the status quo.

- Get your people's mind off themselves and onto a worthy objective, one that can be measured.

- Motivation to accomplish results tends to increase when people have meaningful goals toward which to work.

- Higher exceptions generally lead to higher performance. Lower expectations generally lead to lower performance.

- When cooperation is not forthcoming after a reasonable time, require compliance with career disturbing consequences for those who fail to get the message.

- Require subordinate managers to develop subordinate goals and objectives with SMART; S- Specific, M-Measurable, A-Attainable, R-Realistic, T-Time based (Specific time frames and deadlines)

- Keep them informed as to how the organization is progressing and how their contributions are influencing that progress.

Morale, Motivation & Discipline, – Running a tight ship

Like the elements of fire; oxygen, fuel, and heat, so productivity in management is made up of morale, motivation and discipline. Take away one element and the fire goes out. Morale is the oxygen, the breath of life, the spirit of the individual employee and the organization itself. Motivation is the fuel, the wind in the sails of the individual and the organization. Discipline is the heat that tempers steel or melts it, depending on how it needs to be administered. When they themselves are not receiving expected benefits and needed encouragement employees' motivation may be directed against the organization or its managers. All three elements must be sustained together if productivity is to be realized. It follows then that if any of the three elements is missing or lacking it will adversely affect the others.

Discipline: It is easy to see why the ships company was in such a demoralized state. There is no discipline. Discipline is the single most significant element in the makeup of morale. Discipline is the maintenance of pre-established standards against which to measure our own performance. There are standards of performance, dress, behavior, production, safety and so on. The ability to achieve standards of performance provides and maintains an environment for achievement through worthwhile work. Achieving or exceeding these standards creates pride in ones' self and in the organization. More on discipline later in this chapter.

Morale: The emotional state, mental condition, disposition, spirit or mood of an individual, or group with respect to courage, cheerfulness, confidence, enthusiasm, loyalty and self-discipline.

Dwight D. Eisenhower, in the position of Supreme Allied Commander made this statement: *"Morale is at one and the same time the strongest and the most delicate of growths. It withstands shocks and disasters on the battlefield, but can be utterly destroyed by favoritism, neglect and injustice."* When organizations fail to maintain standards of behavior, performance and productivity and fail to recognize it, it is perceived as neglect or injustice. General George Patton once said *"morale is important to every unit . . . It is the spirit of those who follow and the spirits of those who lead that gain the victory"*

The life breath, the oxygen, and the spirit each individual brings to the organization combine with other to create organizational morale. The morale of individuals and groups is determined by the opinions of themselves as individuals, in the association with fellow peers, the organization's managers, and the perceived status of the job they perform. We can see by the lack of positive motivation that morale is not very high. The wind has gone out of their sails.

The first element in morale is discipline. None of the conditions of morale can exist without standards against which to measure and to which individuals and organizations strive.

When the standards of discipline are no longer important and no one is concerned with maintaining standards and they become absurd, the breath goes out of the operation. When there is no morale there is no motivation or desire to engage the emotional energy necessary to make a contribution.

Training plays an important role in morale. The captain made a big deal out of insisting that all departments post the GTMO training exercise schedule for all ships company to see. He insisted that training for those exercises begin immediately. We can easily see that, if the captain was to raise the morale of the crew, they had to have meaningful objectives for which to strive. Once they began training for the exercise their competence would improve, their confidence, not only in themselves, but in the future of the ship and consequently morale would improve.

The reputation of the organization is another significant factor in morale. The perception of status in the eyes of others in the organization and outside the organization affects morale. Oddly enough their perception of the boss' status and reputation in the eyes of the higher ups is a contributing factor in the morale of the crew. Other elements include competent management and worthwhile work. Jobs have purpose and its contribution to the organization's mission is apparent. Camaraderie in the workgroup is a key element in morale. People need people. It is important that people in the workforce regard each other with respect.

Motivation:
Motivation is that inner drive or personal desire to take some purposeful action in the hope of accomplishing or experiencing a worthwhile outcome. This is the wind in the sails, the fuel that keeps the propulsion going. Without motivation or the incentive to perform no one would commit to the task at hand or practice the discipline necessary to accomplish anything. When there is no discipline and morale is low a counter motivation condition is created. Counter motivation are actions employees and lower level management levies against the company as punishment for making them feel inferior.

Discipline:
Webster's New World Dictionary defines discipline as "***Training that develops self-control, character, and orderly conduct***". To the executive discipline is **the maintenance of pre-established standards.**

Employees are made aware of the standards, they are trained to meet those standards and they are continually held accountable for maintaining those standards.

The conduct of well-disciplined employees is the result of training that has caused them to accept and live according to certain behavior patterns. In most cases, where a person has had extensive training in some professional discipline, or a highly skilled trade self-discipline is almost automatic when morale and motivation are present.

We have discovered that Morale and motivation stand on the foundation of discipline. Without discipline, or the maintenance of standards, there is no routine, no regimentation, and no penchant for appropriateness. Without discipline, anarchy prevails. Anarchy breeds confusion, conflict, frustration, and defeat.

Discipline is the foundation for productivity. Discipline represents the ultimate product of good leadership in developing group solidarity, esprit, motivation and skillful performance. Discipline is the individual or group attitude that insures prompt obedience to orders and initiation of appropriate actions in the absence of orders.

By creating a climate of discipline one in which orders are rational, and consistently enforced and with regular realistic performance evaluation and taking appropriate action to correct behavior that does not meet the established standard, or rewarding those that exceed it.

Maintaining discipline calls for disciplinary action. Disciplinary action is any action taken to maintain cognizance of the standards. To illustrate this point, we use boundary lines to show optimum standards, a level above which we would appreciate but do not normally expect, and minimum standards, the absolute lowest performance, or behavior we will tolerate. These standards could mean anything; behavior standards, performance standards, attendance, or any situation where one would be expected to conduct themselves appropriately.

Optimum standard

Minimum Standard

Most employees operate somewhere between the two boundaries.

When employees violate or fall short of some standard, the manager takes corrective action or "disciplinary action". Not so much to punish, but to train and encourage, helping them come back up to the standard. More often than not this is done by providing additional information or training followed by monitored performance for a period.

Disciplinary action should be "uplifting." Of course when the subordinate manager continues to operate below the standard after training and counseling does not work action with a greater consequence is called for. Now is the time for reprimand and warnings that continued, below par performance, will result in a strained relationship with the company, and maybe even result in the end of the employer - employee relationship. When an employee rises above the standard we take "disciplinary action". Not to punish, but to recognize, reward, train and encourage, helping them maintain the new standard. Disciplinary action should be "uplifting."

Management Axioms:

- Never allow unsatisfactory work to go unchallenged.
- Never let good work or behavior go unrecognized.
- Never let outstanding work or behavior go unrewarded.
- Never hesitate to take the action necessary.
- The highest level of performance you can expect is the lowest level of performance you will settle for.

Rule of Command #3

There is always a cause that prompts every action. Find and eliminate the causes of misconduct and poor performance.

Rule of Command #4

Do not delay taking disciplinary action, whether to correct or reward. The longer you wait the less impact it will have.

Chapter 3

**Collision Course
Friday, 06 March 1970
Offices of the Benchmark Consulting Group
Silver Spring, Maryland**

1500: The drill weekend was to commence on Friday 13, March. In the late afternoon of Thursday 6, March, Captain Mills made an unannounced visit to the ship. For the past four weeks, Robert Mills spent most of his time at his corporate office. He had inherited a competent, well trained staff and two very good junior consultants that would someday be offered a partnership in the firm. There was always two or three Master's and Ph.D. candidate interns involved in the operations who proved to be valuable assets to those engaged in projects. This month a Ph.D. candidate from George Mason University was on board. Students from George Mason were usually top level consultants who caught on quickly. All Ph.D. graduates from that school were offered big jobs in the government. This one was seeking a position with the Navy Department. Mills made arrangements for an extended absence as he would need to spend time on the ship piloting a reluctant officer corps.

Lt. Winthrop met him at that office or accepted invitations to lunch in order to keep the Captain supplied with the information he had specified he wanted on a periodic basis. The Captain also met with Lieutenant Commander McCormick every Thursday evening to get his reports. Winthrop and McCormick treated Commander Mills with deference but also with stiff formality.

Captain Mills noted that progress was being made in establishing some routines for maintenance and repairs, and the administrative and operational files were improving. The assessments, submitted by the department heads, were incomplete and contained little or no tactical or specific plans for achieving operational readiness. The problem facing the officers of the *Card*, Mills thought, is the lack of supervision. Too much independence breeds discomfort. Everyone needs to know that someone is requiring accountability.

Now here he was standing on the pier admiring the ship, as he always does. He was in uniform and carried an overnight bag in his hand. There was her name *CARD* standing out in relief from the after part of the hull, highlighted by the white paint on her letters. "How can one not be proud of any ship they are assigned to?" he thought. He walked up the gang plank, stopping at the brow. He noticed the quarter deck watch and the O.O.D. were wearing dress blues. He rendered a salute to the Ensign (American flag) flying on the fantail. He then turned to face the quarterdeck officer and saluted.

"Request permission to come aboard."

The Officer of the Deck (OOD) was Ensign Nick Winchester. "Permission granted," he said, and he returned his salute.

Commander Mills stepped on to the quarterdeck. The quarterdeck watch keyed the ship's broadcast microphone and announced; "*USS CARD* arriving." *Note: The commanding officer is formally identified by position not rank and name.*

Lieutenant Winthrop hurried aft to meet the Captain. He rendered a salute and said, "Welcome aboard, Sir. We weren't expecting you until tomorrow morning."

The Captain returned his salute. "I wanted to check on our preparations for the drill weekend," the Captain responded. "Have the yeoman get the command logs and other records lined up for my review. I'd like to begin with them." *Note: Saluting seniors is not necessary aboard ship, as the senior officer afloat receives and returns the salute from the OOD each morning. This salute obviates the need for any further saluting which could be cumbersome in many onboard situations.*

"I'll do that right away, Captain." Winthrop paused, and then added, "Before the Captain gets too involved in the details of our preparations may I have a private word?"

The Captain nodded. "Certainly, I'm on my way up to my cabin now. If you'd like to walk along with me..." He turned and proceeded up the ladder, by the stack on the O-4 level and forward into the skin of the ship. Winthrop followed at his heels, and Captain Mills spoke over his shoulder to the Lieutenant as they went.

"When was the last time you ran a Title B inventory?"

"It's only been a matter of weeks," answered the Lieutenant, "I'd have to check the files to be able to give the Captain an exact date, though."

"I'd like to see that along with the command logs. Are the registered publications up to date?"

"I'm quite certain that they are, Sir."

"I don't think they are, Lieutenant. I want your Senior Petty Officers working on them during this drill weekend. It makes no sense for us to be trying to get this vessel in sea-worthy shape if we don't even have the proper specifications of what that shape is. Also, it will be good training for the reserves."

"Aye, aye, Captain," Winthrop replied laconically.

"I also want the transport and stores report ready."

Before Winthrop could reply, Captain Mills entered his cabin. He noticed several articles of clothing and other personal items on the bed and table. Without looking back at the Lieutenant he asked; "whose gear is this?"

"It's mine, Sir. Since the Captain only uses the cabin one weekend out of the month, I stay here and move to my own stateroom during drill weekends."

Mister Winthrop had tried to give his reply in as off-handed a manner as he could. "With you or Captain Gallagher only on board a few times a month for department head meetings and reserve crew weekends, I like to maintain a command presence here so the men will be used to coming up here for a decision." Captain Mills didn't answer right away, so Winthrop continued his pitch.

"You have a civilian business to run, and you don't need the additional worries about the day-to-day operation of the *Card*. You can leave everything to me, Sir. Besides, the officers and men are used to me."

The Captain was now facing Lieutenant Winthrop and looking at him directly. He spoke in a posture and tone that surprised the Lieutenant that Mills' voice was neither loud nor harsh. But it was clear and firm.

"Mister Winthrop, my responsibility for this ship is not diminished when you assume OIC duties. I am still accountable for it. I'm responsible every hour of the day. I am responsible for the condition of this ship, the daily production, the conduct of the crew and for the quality of the training that goes on. That responsibility is in effect at all times."

"That may be true," Mister Winthrop replied, not yet deterred, "but we do have an unusual situation. I am the Officer in Charge when you're not here, and you're not here most of the time. In that case, I have to assume most of the leadership."

Captain Mills continued to hold his face and voice in check. "Yes, Mister Winthrop, you are the OIC when I'm not around, but I am the Commanding Officer at <u>all</u> times. Your responsibility is to carry out my orders, and you must know <u>that</u> is what you are going to be held accountable for."

The OIC wasn't yet ready to give up the contest. "I don't think the Captain has any reason to doubt that I will follow his orders. I'm every bit as committed as you are to the job of getting the *Card* back into shape, seaworthy and combat-ready."

The Captain was losing a degree of his composure. "I'm getting the disturbing impression, Mister Winthrop, that you're more concerned about your status than you are about the needs of this ship. As a leader, you will have to be committed to the needs of the organization. You need a sense of purpose that goes beyond simply being the one in charge. You must understand Lieutenant that the organization is the goose that lays the golden eggs. Our job, as leaders of this organization, is to take care of the goose."

He stood facing him. Expressionless, he took a long pregnant pause, a pause that created no small degree of anxiety in the OIC. Exactly what the Captain had intended. "The organization's leaders are not the kings, the organization is the king. Its leaders are the stewards of the organization's resources, the natural custodian of its future, its reputation, its mission, its stability, and the people assigned to it". The Captain leaned against the desk, folded his arms across his chest and continued. "Leadership requires a strong sense of self, to be sure, but an appropriate sense of self.

There must be a willingness to assume command but not for one's own benefit, but the benefit of the organization and its members. To do that properly the leader must have a clear vision of the mission, and a sense of stewardship. And something, I think you are lacking, is a sense of follower-ship, not just the follower-ship of those who report to you, but willingness to assume the follower-ship of those to whom you report."

The Captain scanned the OIC's personal belongings stacked neatly around the cabin. It appeared the Lieutenant had taken up residence.

"Something else you need to learn, Lieutenant. The Boss' office is sacred territory, no one should occupy that space until they have earned it and have been properly assigned to it. You are the Officer in Charge, you are not the Captain."

He could see the frustration on the OIC's face. "You have something to say Mister Winthrop?"

The challenge had come out into the open, and Winthrop responded; "Honestly?"

"Mister Winthrop I do not ask questions expecting to get a dishonest answer. If you have something you want to say to me, say it."

"Permission to speak frankly Sir."

"Certainly."

"Captain, with all due respect - and I'd never say this in front of the other officers - I know what it's like to have command of a military vessel. I have been in charge of this ship for some time now; I have experience in running this organization and I think I have a good understanding of what's best for all concerned. If you come in now and remove my authority right away, well, Sir, I think we'll have some real problems on this ship."

Captain Mills' voice and gaze were still level when he replied, "With all due respect? I saw no due respect in your statement, Mister Winthrop. And what you think about the way I command this ship is irrelevant. You have provided me with your assessment. That will be all. I'll call you if I need you."

Mister Winthrop hesitated a minute to consider whether he wanted to challenge the Captain's comment about no respect, but better judgment prevailed and he decided to let it go. "I'll just move my gear to my space." said Winthrop, beginning to edge around the Captain toward the bed.

The Captain didn't move, but instead simply said, "I'll have my Steward bring them to you. You're dismissed, Mr. Winthrop."
"Sir, your Steward is a reserve and won't come on board until tomorrow night. I'll need my belongings before then."

"I said you're dismissed Mr. Winthrop. That will be all."

The Captain had wanted to avoid a confrontation with Mr. Winthrop. He was not prepared, at that moment, to take on heavy seas with him.

Although the OIC was not a polished executive like his high ranking ancestors, it was never the less true that his energy was great, his ability to secure commitment from others undoubted, he apparently had connections with top Navy brass, and his tenacity was such that no administrator was willing to disturb him-- a bad man to have against you.

Friday, 13 March 1970
Reserve Drill Weekend
USS Card Pier Side
US Coast Guard Yard, Curtis Bay Maryland

1000: When the drill weekend commenced on 13 March it was soon apparent they would be unable to get underway that weekend also. The inlet to the engine cooling system kept clogging and the uncertain flow ran the risk of losing power or damaging the turbine. An additional problem was, again, that many of the enlisted reserves were absent. The Captain ordered the XO to send a memorandum to all *USS Card* reserve personnel, informing them of their contract obligations to the US Navy in general and the *USS Card* in particular. Absences without prior approval will be considered Absence Without Leave (AWOL) and disciplinary action will be taken. The memo also stated absence will adversely affect their retirement points.

While there were no visible signs of disrespect or insubordination. The officers and crew treated the Captain with stiff properness. They offered strict compliance but very little active cooperation. Their treatment of Mr. Winthrop was one of familiar deference and over-zealous consideration, giving the appearance that they considered Mr. Winthrop their skipper.

Normal ship board activities continued according to the structure of naval ships moored to a pier.

1000: The Captain informed the Executive Officer that he expected each department to conduct combat drills.

1015: General Quarters was sounded and the department heads struggled through some combat exercises, but the entire matter was not pretty. The sailors did not like the exercises and did not hesitate to complain loudly.

1150: The 1-MC blasted the eleven fifty routine. "Now, Quartermaster reports. Chronometers wound and compared to OOD. Now, twelve O'clock reports. Permission to strike eight bells to the Captain."

Eight Bells was struck.

1200: The voice over the 1-MC made the noon announcement "Now pipe to dinner."

1300: The Executive Officer requested a stand down from the GQ drills offering the Captain an alternative. Each department head will conduct an assessment of the morning drills and determine corrective measures for future drills.

The Captain agreed but insisted on written reports delivered to him before 1800 hours this evening.

1600: Mister Goldsmith had informed the Captain that the banners with the ship's coat of arms were hanging in the mess deck as ordered. He went down to see how it was displayed. The banner was about four feet high and six feet wide, tacked up on the forward bulkhead where all who entered would see it.

Across the top were the embroidered words; *U.S.S. Card (DE 383)*. In the center was the coat of arms. The ship's motto was written in Latin across a waving banner strip. Under the coat of arms was the motto in English; "Seek – Strike – Prevail."

Seaman Jones of the reserve crew was standing behind the serving counter as the Captain studied the banner. "Is that who we are Captain?" he asked.

"Yes Jonesey that's who we are," He answered.

1715: The duty Boatswain mate of the watch keyed the 1-MC and made an important announcement. "Supper is now being served on the mess decks."

17:30 Department heads issued the *Card's* coat-of-arms patches to each enlisted sailor and officers. They were instructed to sew this patch on their work jackets. They were allowed to take up to five extra patches for their civilian jackets if they wanted them.

Almost every enlisted sailor took the advantage of the five extra patches. The ship's identification patch was issued to all the enlisted with directions to have them sewn on dress and undress blues and whites in time for the April drill weekend.

They were told there would be a sea bag inspection during the April drill weekend and to ensure the patches were in place. (*Undress blues are winter uniforms without a tie or the white piping. Undress whites are the summer white uniforms without the tie*).

1800: The evening of 13 March found Captain Mills working late at the desk in his cabin. Piles of folders covered much of the desk, table, bed and floor. Sheets of yellow legal-pad notepaper on which the Captain had recorded his ideas and plans topped off each pile. A knock on the door prompted the Captain to turn in the direction of the knock. Lieutenant Commander McCormick was standing in the doorway.

"Lieutenant Commander McCormick requests permission to speak to the Captain."

"Certainly, Commander" Captain Mills replied, pushing his chair back from the desk.

He cleared two piles of folders from the other chair, and motioned to his Executive Officer to take a seat in the space he had just cleared. "Please, have a seat. I'm glad you're here."

It was clear that the Executive Officer had come with the purpose of making a statement, but was quite uncomfortable. "Captain, I'd like to say again, on behalf of all the officers and men on the *Card,* that we really appreciate all the things you're trying to do to get the ship back into combat-ready status, and how you're trying to get everyone started in the right direction on these projects." He was still beating around the proverbial bush, and the Captain let him go.

"But, Sir, I did want to discuss one other thing with you. Before we get too far with this, "Get Well" program, I have to express some reservations I have about the way certain things are going."

Mills leaned back in his chair and looked as if he was studying the Exec, but he didn't say anything.

"Captain, I'm quite concerned about the relationship you're developing with Lieutenant Winthrop," he continued, still tentatively. "I'd hate to have the two of you continue to get off in different directions." The XO spoke hesitatingly, hoping that the Captain would break in with some statement of his own; an agreement he could build on or an objection that could be refuted. However the Captain said nothing and only remained looking impassively at him, so the Exec continued.

"With all due respect, Captain, I think the main problem is that you're mis-reading the Lieutenant. He's a good officer. It would be difficult to find a man better qualified to be in control of this ship while us reserve types are back at our civilian jobs."

The Captain said nothing but sat with his arms across his chest and his eyes focused on the visitor's face.

"Sir, Lieutenant Winthrop has earned the respect and the loyalty of the officers and enlisted men of this ship. I recommend a gradual change in the way things are done. Don't change things overnight. I'm quite sure the men will all come to both feel and show a great deal of respect for you as well, once they've become more comfortable with the Captain's style and, well, mannerisms."

He waited for a response but there was none, and no change of expression.

"I am just…recommending that you cut Mister Winthrop some slack, I think that if you treat him with a little more respect, the rest of us would feel a bit more comfortable. Things will go a lot smoother, if you could get on the good side of Mr. Winthrop, he carries a lot of weight with the crew. Captain Gallagher believed in sharing leadership. Perhaps if you shared leadership with Mr. Winthrop and me . . . well maybe our comfort level will allow us to take a greater role in this ship's disposition."

Their train of thought was interrupted by the shrill whistle of the boatswain's pipe followed by the loud sound of the boatswain making an announcement over the ship's PA system.

"Now . . . attention to colors."

The Captain looked at his watch it was Eighteen-thirty, sundown. He held up his hand indicating that he wanted no further talking until after colors. There was the blaring sound of a trumpet playing "retreat" as topside the National Ensign was being lowered by the quarterdeck watch, The Officer of the Day on the quarterdeck and all hands within sight of the flag stood at attention and saluted. All other hands within the ship stood silent.

When the trumpet's retreat was ended the boatswain piped carry on and then announced **"Carry On."**

The Captain turned his attention again to LDCR McCormick and said; "Commander McCormick, I am under the impression that your concept of Captain is different from mine. I believe in sharing leadership Mr. McCormick. I believe in sharing management through the delegation of authority. I don't believe in sharing command. Captain Gallagher shared command and you see where that got you. There can only be one skipper. Believe me Mr. McCormick; I will expect you and Mr. Winthrop to assume your share of leadership."

The XO pushed his better judgment aside and pressed on. "Up to now, I think morale's been pretty high, but..." his voice trailed off. He reached behind the flap on the inside cover of his notebook and removed a piece of notepaper, which had apparently been torn from a bulletin board. "I've started seeing signs of trouble we've never had before on the *Card*. I think you ought to be aware of them before things get too far out of hand."

Captain Mills took the scrap of paper. Across the top, someone had printed the notice: "EFFECTIVE IMMEDIATELY! The beatings will continue until morale improves!"

"Commander McCormick, everyone who becomes a ship's Captain brings to that job his own philosophy of command." He looked up to face his Executive Officer. "That philosophy is the sum total of everything he's read, seen, heard or thought. We read textbooks on leadership, we've sat through lectures and seminars on command, watched our superiors succeed or fail by their actions." He leaned forward. "We observe our own attempts turn out well or poorly. Through all these experiences, we've each developed our own thoughts and ideas concerning the proper way to command a ship." He paused to make sure Mr. McCormick was keeping up with him.

"In any organization, there can be only one single direction taken. If an organization begins to pull in more than one direction, energy is taken from accomplishment of its mission and dissipated in internal friction."

The Captain leaned back in his chair and crossed his legs, hanging his left leg over his right knee. "In the Navy, we have much less allowance for error than most other organizations. We have to operate under extraordinary conditions much of the time; decisions not only have to be correct, but have to be timely and carried out immediately. We simply have less of a margin for error."

He paused but he did not take his eyes off the officer's face. After a few seconds, that felt like an hour to the man sitting across from him. The Captain continued.

"And because of that, it's vital that we follow the principle of 'Unity of Command'; simple, clear-cut lines of authority. We can have only one person in command of this ship, and since I've been designated that person, I intend to exercise my authority to fulfill my responsibilities." Captain Mills paused again for effect. He was looking straight into Mister McCormick's eyes. He continued.

"My responsibilities are clear: Get the *Card* back into combat-ready condition, get the crew functioning as a combat-capable unit, and have us join the rest of the squadron for the exercises off Guantanamo in July. If you feel that the crew in general or Mister Winthrop in specific aren't fully aware of my philosophy and my goals, then maybe that's an area where I need to focus more of my attention. On the other hand, if you're suggesting that I change my thoughts and ideas on command to more closely match those of a former commander, I would only reply that I was given command of this ship for a specific purpose and for what ComResDesRon saw as certain qualities in my philosophy."

The Captain placed both feet flat on the floor and leaned in close to his Executive Officer. "You are my second in command, Mike, my chief of staff. If I can't rely on you, then perhaps we need to have a serious talk about your future with the *Card*." He paused again and let out an audible breath. He sat back in his chair and continued "and your future with the Navy."

"That will not be necessary Captain."

"That's fine my boy, then we don't have a problem do we?"

Saturday, 14 March 1970
Reserve Drill Weekend
USS Card Pier Side
US Coast Guard Yard, Curtis Bay Maryland

0700: The winters in Baltimore were bitter cold. Any work done on the weather decks required foul weather jackets and cold weather head gear. The weather in March was wet, not as cold but still very uncomfortable for the crew who lined up on the weather decks, by department, at their abandon ship stations for early morning muster. The discomfort did not seem to be the focus of discontent now, as it had been in late November, December and January.

The officers had returned from Officers Call and were standing before their subordinates. They spoke in low tones so as not to disturb the other units. If one listened carefully they could hear the water splashing against the hull, as the tide, on its inexorable movement went out to sea. And there was the smell of the diesel fumes and the stench of the back waters of the Chesapeake Bay combined with a foul odor wafting across the bay from the manufacturing plants on the other side.

There was a new officer standing with Mister Hooper in front of the Deck Division. "Ladies and Gentlemen this is Lieutenant (j.g.) Foster Gilliam. He is with the reserve force at the Philadelphia Navy Yard. He is assigned to the *USS Granger.* He will be going to Guantanamo with us. He is visiting here as a sort of recon mission." They all smiled at the idea of recon, but that is exactly what it was. No self-respecting leader wants surprises, and Forster Gilliam is one who wants to know, beforehand, what he will be encountering.

"I appreciate the opportunity to sail with you during the combat exercises. I served two years on the *USS Bevard (DD 827),* before going to inactive reserves. The Gitmo cruise will be my first since returning to ready reserve status."

"Mister Gilliam." One of the reserve seamen apprentices (E-2) called out. "How did you get stuck with this tub?" Several of the others chimed in with utterances related to the question. "Well as luck would have it, all the billets on the *Granger* were filled. There was a billet for an officer on the *Card*, I was offered it and I took it."

"I doubt luck is the right word, Sir," said another seaman, from the regular Navy ship's company. "I would say bad luck. This barge has the worst reputation in the fleet, reserve or regular."

Mister Gilliam raised the volume of his voice when he replied; "Is it your belief that this ship has a bad reputation? I submit to you people this ship has done nothing to warrant a bad reputation."

Officers and crew from the surrounding muster stations heard the increased volume of the visiting officer's voice and tuned their ears to hear what was being said.

"The reputation of any organization is created by the crew that mans her. If you want a ship with a good reputation, then you must provide the level of commitment and competence that will result in that level of honor. I am proud to have the opportunity to serve on the *Card*. I can tell you ladies and gentlemen, I will give this ole girl my best efforts in an attempt to give her a proud reputation. If you will do the same, we may go to Gitmo in disgrace, but we will return in Glory."

As the day unfolded the sailors began to appear at their work stations with the *Card's* coat of arms patch sewn to their work jackets. The general consensus of opinion, among the enlisted, was the coat of arms patch was a good idea and even though they were required to sew it on their work jackets, they were glad to do it.

The Captain once again reminded his Executive Officer he wanted combat drills in each department from 1400 to 1530. The XO passed the word and the crew went about the task, half-heartedly, calling the Capitan a "Captain Blye" like the Captain on the Bounty.

The crew was given liberty at sixteen thirty, and though they were still complaining about the drills, many reserves left the ship with the ship identification patch hastily sewn on the right shoulder of their dress blue uniforms.

Sunday 15, March 1970
Reserve Drill Weekend
USS Card Pier Side
US Coast Guard Yard, Curtis Bay Maryland

It was Zero four-hundred (4:00 AM) when Captain Mills left his cabin. He stepped out onto the 0-4 weather deck and descended an 8 step ladder on to the 0-3 level by the stack. It was a custom with Robert Mills. It was a time of quiet solitude. The type of solitude that could only be experienced topside on a ship at sea. It was a bit blustery, but his deck jacket provided sufficient warmth against the wind. He walked to the edge of the deck facing east.

He placed a foot up on the second rung of the railing that surrounded the deck and focused on a set of running lights passing in the night, far out past the channel in the open sea. A ship was going somewhere, with a well-trained crew no doubt. He felt a presence near him on the right.

"By your leave Captain."

The Captain turned slightly toward the voice. "Granted." It was First Class Petty Officer Boatswain's (boats'n) Mate, Ezra Fuhrman. The Captain remembered reading his service file. He was a crusty old salt who for some reason, had left the regular Navy, took a civilian job and joined the Ready Reserves. He volunteered for duty on the *Card*.

"I always come out here at this time," he said. "There is no other time, or place on God's earth quite like it. When I was in the reg-lars on the *Thomas, (DD 831)* in the Caribbean, I made it a habit of going up to the stacks, and spread eagle on the deck and look up at the stars. The deck was always warm against my back. I liked the feel of the vibration of the engines, the sound of the sea splashing against the sides, a gentle warm south-seas breeze wafting across the deck." He paused. "I would just look up and watch the ship's mast move like a pendulum across the stars. I tell you skipper, there ain't a pill in this world that can make you feel that good."

"I know what you mean boats very well said."

"I made a deal with my wife. She said she would stay married to me if I got out. As much as I love being at sea I decided I loved her more, and I did and she did. But I didn't get out entirely. I'm here."

His demeanor changed and he turned his face slightly toward the Captain and in a very different tone he said; "Some of the rinks (*slang for reserve enlisted*) have never been out there. When we get there, they will never forget it. Us old salts (*sailors with a lot of sea time*) are really excited about it. We like the course you're steering."

The Captain dropped his foot, stepped back and turned toward the ladder, with two pats on the old salt's shoulder he said, "Carry on Furman, carry-on." He went back to his cabin.

Chapter 3 Assessment - Collision   Course

Challenges to Authority

Mr. Winthrop is openly challenging the captain's authority. One is compelled to ask "Why is he so blatantly resistive? More often than not, the appearance of new executive in an environment that has been under an interim manager creates a negative reaction when the reigns of command must be relinquished. Mr. Winthrop was the boss and now he sees his position and status as being in jeopardy. It would appear that Mr. Winthrop feels the ambiguity of exerted power and authority. He realizes the Captain's objectives and methods are strikingly different from his. He has had to face the fact that his perception of the organization's mission was different from that of ComResDesRon and that if the Captain is successful he will look like a failure to the crew of the Card.

It appears that Mr. Winthrop, and many of the other officers, have lost sight of their role as subordinate managers. The role of the subordinate manager is to direct the resources under their command toward the accomplishment of their part in the chief executive's vision and mission in the manner set by his stated values. The first element in a manager's code is duty. Duty is a dedication to the service of the organization, the obligations of the position, expressed or implied, coupled with loyalty to designated senior authorities. The manager must resist the temptation for personal ambition and personal comfort at the expense of subordinates' time, talent and the organization's resources.

Top management has the stewardship responsibility to appoint people in critical positions whom they think can best lead the organization to continual, day-to-day mission accomplishment. Sometimes managers are brought in from outside rather than promoting from within the organization. Sometimes the current manager has lost the power to secure and maintain effective performance. Maybe top management and subordinates no longer trust the incumbent's judgment. Top management is no longer satisfied with the direction of the department and prefers a different approach and different management and leadership style. A different style and different climate requires a different manager. It may be the incumbent manager leaves and senior management does not feel the next in line will manage the department effectively. Perhaps the incumbent would use the same style as the predecessor and management does not want that.

The cold hard fact of life, now, is that Robert Mills is in command and a powerful subordinate executive is not cooperating in the transition. When a subordinate manager resists the efforts of the incoming executive, the new manager must deal with the situation head on. This is no time for trying to appease the opponent, it is time for a proactive, not a passive administration. Effective leaders must confront and persuade reluctant others to cooperate or comply with their decisions, whether those others are subordinates, peers, or seniors.

Other members of the management team have their own interests and their own view of situational needs, and either or both of these may cause them to refuse an order or request. Such a refusal can both embarrass and handicap leaders seeking credibility and support.

There is a good reason why this executive is at this level at this time in his career. We do not want to throw him to the sharks, we want him to succeed. The senior executive must provide the resources and training to assist in that success. If he can succeed, he will want to continue in the experience and will realize to remain in this success mode, he will have to cooperate with the boss. Other benefits are readily apparent. The opposition manager will realize that his boss saved him and deserves respect. The affect on morale and the comfort level of other executives and employees is priceless.

The captain said he believed Mr. Winthrop was more interested in his status than the needs of this command. Status is important it is one of the trappings of agency power that assists the manager to influence the behavior and thinking of others. Mr. Winthrop has a strong need for status. He is standing in the shadow of his father, uncle, grandfather and great grandfather. He enjoys the image of being the one in command; he enjoys the trappings of power and status. The Captain needed to show him who was the boss so he dismissed him without letting him collect his things. The subordinate manager needed to experience inconvenience in order for him to realize he has no legitimate claim to the Capitan's position.

Management Axiom

When there is a void in leadership, someone will step in and take charge. The unwillingness to act allows those who are willing to act to prevail. Rivers and people go crooked when they take the path of least resistance.

When subordinates see results through the accomplishment of objectives, they will provide cooperation in order to continue in the success.

Rule of Command #5

When you have tried everything and cooperation cannot be attained, require compliance with consequences for failure to comply.

Rule of Command #6

Management is a contest of wills, persistence is essential if one is to prevail.

Earning Respect and Status

Mr. McCormick advised the Captain to get on the good side of Mr. Winthrop. He implied that he would get the cooperation he was looking for and gain respect at the same time if he would not usurp Mr. Winthrop's authority. Whether they know it or not, the officers and crew of the Card wants someone to step up and provide the means to experience achievement.

Not surprisingly, Mr. Winthrop was occupying the Captain's cabin. The Boss' office is sacred territory, no one should occupy that space until they have earned it and have been properly assigned to it. Donna Kelley served as the assistant Human Resources Manager for the City of Chattanooga from 1977 to 1982. In the fall of 1980, the Human Resources Manager was forced to take medical leave, leaving her to run the operation until his return. For two years she maintained her status as the assistant and conducted the City's personnel business from her own office. When it was evident that her boss would not return, she dutifully assisted in the search for a successor. Ms. Kelley was eventually offered the top HR position, and it was then and only then that she moved into the Executive office. While President Eisenhower was in the hospital recovering from a heart attack, Vice President Nixon ran the presidency from his office in the Executive office building. He did not go into the Oval Office.

When we speak of respect the word honor seems to be required in the definition. The concept of honor is reflected in the term respectable, alluding to a proper self-image, personal fealty, and self-regulating attention to the important. When military honor is effective, its coercive power is considerable, since it persistently points to a single over-riding directive to accomplish the mission with professionalism and dispatch.

The executive gains respect or loses it on three fronts; Respectable character, respect for their command and those in it, and decisive action directed toward the common good of the command. Respect is gained and freely given when that person's character is respectable. One must seek respectability rather than respect. One must be worthy of high regard before one can be respected. One must be decent, proper and correct in character and behavior.

One must have respect for oneself, respect for their God, and respect for others. Military officers are required to be gentlemen and ladies in the noble sense of the word, conforming to high personal standards, and having a sense of propriety.

Civilian executives would do well to imitate this code.

Respect for command is a critical element of respect. Respect for the position calls for a dedication to the service of the organization, the obligations of the position, expressed or implied, coupled with loyalty to designated senior authorities.

When one demonstrates loyalty and respect for the organization and those in it, and those doing business with it they will experience due respect.

Those in authority and power must show a respect for the obligations of position, by carrying out the mission decisively and within a personal and professional code of ethical behavior.

Rule of Command #7

To get respect you must be respectable and give respect.

Management Axiom:

In an organization the senior manager gains respect by decisive action that directs the crew's attention to the accomplishment of a worthwhile task. Inaction earns disrespect.

Controlling Operations

For a ship to reach its destination without sailing off course, the one at the Conn must take frequent bearings. First there must be a plan and a backup plan. There must be an overall strategy and philosophy for work. Plan the work then work the plan. Train and rehearse the plan, plan and rehearse for contingencies, and expect the unexpected. Stick to the plan, and don't lose sight of your mission.

A very significant factor in working the plan and rehearsing for contingencies and to be prepared for the unexpected is a constant and regular measurement of progress. If things are not proceeding according to plans, a corrective action is necessary. Poor control is easy to spot. The manager, who squanders time darting from place to place, checking on everything and everyone, is a victim of his own ineffective controls. Good control with corrective action plans and methods of achieving it is fundamental in the management process.

The job of the manager is to work with people and other resources to accomplish a worthwhile objective for the benefit of the organization. Working with people means that we secure the talents, skills and abilities of others to get that job done. And setting controls to ensure the job is done within specified standards.

It is through the employment of appropriate control that results are attained from the human, technical, material, and organizational resources under the leader's command. Controls that are well designed and properly implemented can have a positive influence on the smooth flow of daily operations. There are basically three types of controls; Pre-controls, in-process controls and post controls.

Effective control methods alert the manager of impending problems within the operation and allow them to make necessary adjustments before the problem gets out of hand, or provide a means of discovering the cause of a problem that is getting out of hand and providing a means to correct it.

Pre-controls or preventive (preliminary) controls are to prevent problems that result from deviations from standard. Safety posters, fire drills, procedures, quality inspections, gauge checking, training of all kinds and Concurrent (in process) controls observe or inspect what is happening (or what has happened) throughout the process and compare these observations (measurements) with the standards of what was supposed to happen.

Next is taking corrective action during the production or delivery process to ensure standards are met. These are your moderately expensive controls.

Post controls (feedback after the process) are evaluations of the activity after it has happened and show problems that need to be addressed for further improvement. The information gained from this feedback control will become one of the pre-controls or concurrent controls for future operations. These are your very expensive controls.

In any management control system the manager must determine whether to use either tight control or loose control. Tight control requires the subordinate to assist in the planning, so critical issues may be addressed. Check points are close together, the degree of decision making is limited and the accountability is strict. It is a good idea to employ tight controls on any new project or situation. It is better to impose slight over control than to risk losing control. It is easier to remove or loosen controls than it is to install them after the project has begun.

Loose control is utilized normally when the subordinate is skilled in the operation. The boss outlines the goals, expected results and deadlines. The subordinate submits a plan of action and a budget. After approval the subordinate reports progress periodically. It is the competency and past experience with the project, not the caliber of the subordinate that determines a tight or loose control situation. Loose control is not abdication. The executive must continue to monitor and maintain responsibility.

The control methods the captain had in place had all the earmarks of a project going bad. The first signs are postponed target dates, vague reports, and a behavior that revealed an attitude of confusion and that nothing was urgent. There was a void of action with regard to the project and a void of action by subordinates will, if tolerated, soon lead to failure to accomplish desired results.

At first glance it may appear that Captain Mills did not put effective controls in place. It would appear that he does not have personal control. One would question why he spent four weeks in his corporate office, and not on the *Card*, receiving reports from his two top managers and not taking charge personally. Perhaps he is using the management rope trick; giving subordinate managers sufficient rope to either hang themselves or swing into success. Most executives use tight control when they first take on an assignment.

When subordinates show they do not need tight control the executive gradually loosens control.

Captain Mills had controls, but they consisted of establishing deadlines for certain events to occur in the rebuilding of each department. He continued to require an assessment report and a get well plan, ready for his attention at a specific time.

He continually stressed the importance of this plan, and the Guantanamo exercises. He put Mr. McCormick and Mr. Winthrop in charge of getting the department head's assessments, but instead of getting the assessments, they gave him vague reports on the progress of the departmental changes without the assessment.

You would think the Captain would have known, by the condition of the ship, that these two officers were either incapable or unwilling to bring the ship to combat readiness. You will recall that this was no normal operational readiness project. The officers and crew were committed to Mr. Winthrop and believed he knew what was best. In this case, and this is an unusual case, Captain Mills needed to expose this traditional thinking for what it was. Effective managers have a real deadline then they set a deadline for their subordinates that will give plenty of time to get the plan worked out and implemented before the actual drop-dead date. Captain Mills was aware that time was fast approaching so he installed a command central for better controlling the "Get Well" project. One would wonder why he waited until March to require this level of control. Most project managers would have set it up when he first announced the project and issued orders to the project team. He gave them a chance to come forward and deliver their assignments on their own. When that did not happen and it appeared that the deadlines would not be met he established this absolute control mechanism.

Since he was not getting cooperation with his plan and compliance was dragging, it was time to take charge to do something drastic. He needs to get down to the action and take control personally. The greatest potential for control exists at the point where the action takes place. Since it was obvious to all by now that there wasn't enough time or commitment it was time to call in outside services to assist in getting the ship out to sea. It would be an embarrassment to the leaders of the operation, but it had to be done. He needed to get the ship underway, or at least try. Their experience at sea would be the cold shower shock that will get them working on the real plan to outfit the ship and crew for Guantanamo Bay. If that did not do it, he was prepared to replace every ineffective manager on board.

Some control methods require pertinacity, the tenacity to keep pertinent issues in motion, combined with the determination to see the mission through at all costs, with doggedness and patience. This especially relevant in situations where disaster is the consequence for continuing current practices, the executive must place one action before all others and insist on a successful outcome. This requires will-power and discipline. Without will power and discipline the effort cannot be sustained. That one action in this case, is to get the *Card* underway.

Then there's *Management by Exception*. It is used only in organizations with a competent staff and smooth operations. When the senior manager is juggling multiple projects some operations do not get full attention. Those operations that do not need constant attention are placed in the management by exception category. They get attention when something is not right or when things are very right and rewards are in order.

Rule of Command #8

You do not need to control how people do their jobs, you control what and when. In the final analysis the subordinate manager must be able to get results on their own, using their own methods.

Management Axioms:

- If you tie a subordinate manager down doing a job your way, you tie yourself up making sure it is done your way.

- If after a reasonable time to act has not produced progress toward results, then get down to the scene of operation, personally convene relevant personnel and don't adjourn until measurable objectives have been established, expected outcomes have been identified, strategies for completion have been made, personnel have been delegated to carry out those strategies and measurable activities are underway. And make a note to loosen the pin of those who failed to act.

- Assign activities or projects to the appropriate person.

- Performance does not come from what you expect, but from what you inspect!

Chapter 4

General Quarters
Tuesday, 17 March 1970
USS Card Pier Side
US Coast Guard Base Curtis Bay, Maryland

0900: Captain Mills was aware that time was fast approaching since he was not getting cooperation with his plan and compliance was dragging, it was time to take charge to do something drastic. He decided he needed to get down to the action and take control personally. The greatest potential for control exists at the point where the action takes place. Since it was obvious to all by now that there wasn't enough time or commitment it was time to call in outside services to assist in getting the ship out to sea. It would be an embarrassment to the leaders of the operation, but it had to be done. He needed to get the ship underway, or at least try. Their experience at sea would be the cold shower shock that will get them working on the real plan to outfit the ship and crew for Guantanamo Bay. If that did not do it, he was prepared to replace every ineffective manager on board.

Realizing that he was too far removed from the situation on the ship, Captain Mills moved into his stateroom on board the *Card* so he could personally supervise the ships company and selected reserves in preparing the ship for getting underway for the next drill weekend.

Wednesday, 18 March 1970
USS Card
Pier Side
US Coast Guard Base Curtis Bay, Maryland

0900: The Captain called a special meeting of the ship's officers to discuss the status of the project. None of the reserve officers objected to coming in on their "off duty" time to get instructions and direction from the Captain about the Gitmo cruise. By now they all realized the Captain was serious and they had better get with the program or face consequences they did not want to think about. After all this was the Navy! The meeting began immediately after morning colors.

"I am not satisfied with the progress of our assessments and plans so I will personally take charge. The wardroom will be our command central. The civilians call it the visibility room. It is a central information and status report repository where all information and progress is posted for all to see."

He pointed to a project control chart he had installed on the port bulkhead (wall) over the hat shelf. "We will use this Gantt chart to track our progress." He had placed the master plan on the shelf past where the hats are placed.

"This is where we will meet to discuss the project, and I expect each of you to bring your plans here, and track your part on the chart. I think it would be easier to monitor our progress if each of you entered your own data. By watching changes in inputs and processes time will then be available to take corrective action."

The meeting continued up to lunch when the Captain took a break to allow the stewards to prepare the table and set out the meal. When all was in order, the officers sat down for the meal but continued to discuss the project.

1800: After the officer's meeting, Captain Mills called Mr. Winthrop to the bridge and instructed him to secure the necessary requisitions from the ship's officers and personally deliver them to NAVBASE. "Your job is to ride herd on these requisitions and get them processed. I want them all filled and available on board in time for the next drill weekend."

Captain Mills spent a brief time watching work on the cooling system, but felt his presence was having an inhibiting effect on the workers. He examined other areas in the engineering spaces, noted their condition and the level of work, and then looked for the Engineering Officer. He found Lt. Fridel sitting at the console of the Engineering Watch writing reports on his petty officers. The Captain asked the Lieutenant to accompany him up to his cabin.

"Mr. Fridel," the Captain began when they were both seated, "I've just spent an hour looking at the engine room, boiler plant, diesel generator compartment and most of your other spaces. Frankly they're all a mess. I don't think your cleanup program is working too well."

The Lieutenant returned his gaze without emotion. Captain Mills continued.

"In the first place, there's an oily residue over just about everything; greasy dust on most surfaces. How can you expect people to work in such filth? You've got overflowing trash cans in every compartment, tools are just lying around."

"The men have been busy trying to get the systems back in operation," Mr. Fridel tried to explain. "It happens with a lot of overhaul work; things come out in worse condition than they were before."

"Specifically, which systems?" Captain Mills had pulled out a notebook and was prepared to write in it.

Mr. Fridel shrugged. "Basically all of the major ones; steam generation, turbine, fuel pumps, primary and back-up electrical generators."

"And have you identified these in writing like I asked you to?" the Captain asked with a raised eyebrow.

"I was going to work on those plans tomorrow morning or afternoon at the latest," the Lieutenant replied.

"And are you clear on what items I'm looking for in those plans?"

"I think so, Sir."

"I'm expecting each area to be identified separately, and to have both an accurate description of the problems and a detailed get-well plan. And your recovery plan should list required parts, tools and outside assistance, and it needs to have realistic time-lines for the accomplishment of all tasks."

"I understand that, Captain, but Lt. Winthrop made a good point. If we put in all the necessary requisitions, there will be a lot of embarrassing questions asked. It's going to be tough to answer a lot of them."

"It's going to be even tougher if we have to explain why we missed going on the exercise to GITMO for a third year in a row." Mills had put down his pen and was leaning across the table, looking directly at the Engineering Officer. "Everyone on this ship has to remember what's most important. Right now that's getting underway. You worry about that; I'll deal with any embarrassing questions that might come up." He sat back.

"So you are going to work on the plans later on this afternoon?"

"Whenever the Captain's through with me here," Mr. Fridel replied.

The Captain ignored the implication. "Which system will you begin with?" He asked.

"All of them, I guess."

"I doubt you'll be able to work that way," Mills shook his head. "I suggest you begin on the boilers. They're keeping us from energizing any of the other systems. We don't even know what else we've got wrong. Break it down even further. The fuel subsystem ought to be treated in a report of its own: Inspect all the critical areas, identify problems; order equipment, tools and parts as necessary, and schedule the work to get done."

The Captain continued for a short while, but observed that Lt. Fridel had only nodded in agreement. He had not taken notes nor asked a single question. Captain Mills decided he needed to monitor events in Engineering for himself for now.

Thursday, 19 March 1970
USS Card Pier Side
US Coast Guard Base Curtis Bay, Maryland

1000: When he returned to the engine room, Captain Mills asked a few preliminary questions of the technicians working on the cooling system, but generally tried to remain in the background. As he observed work on that system, he overheard other noises coming from the upper level.

Someone was obviously making more progress describing the ancestry of a piece of equipment than he was at repairing it. Mills decided to investigate. In an awkward position, straining to make an adjustment on a steam fitting, he discovered the Engineman Senior Chief Walter Gruber. (ENCS)

"Good morning, Chief," the Captain announced his presence.

"What's good about it?" the Chief responded.

"What's good about it," the Captain answered, "is that there is someone actually working on something important."

"Oh, Captain, I beg your pardon," The Chief said as he stepped out from behind the steam plant.

"What's the problem in this area?" Mills continued.

"You see, Sir," Gruber was now out from behind the unit and wiping his hands on a rag, "when the system's been out of commission as long as this a whole bunch of things go wrong. It's just like leaving your car parked for two or three months. In the case of a steam system like this, the gaskets dry out. We won't know how many need adjusting or changing out until we get the steam flowing and get up to full pressure."

The Captain nodded as he looked around. "I don't see anyone helping you, Chief. Where are the other Enginemen?"

"The way this valve's situated, they couldn't do much except get in the way."

"Couldn't someone other than a Chief work on it?"

The Chief looked at Captain Mills. He was going to speak directly. "There isn't that many Enginemen I'd trust to work on these valves. We've been trying to keep them qualified on a number of tasks, but I just can't trust them on something as critical as this. This system operates on 1,200 PSI of steam, superheated to around 800 degrees. It doesn't take much of a mistake before you have guys killed." He paused. "That's how we lost three of them on the *Roberts* a few years ago."

The Captain nodded again. Things like that haunted everyone in command. "But we can't keep on doing business this way, Chief. It's not good for you, for the men, nor for the ship. We need to get them qualified and be able to trust them."

The Chief agreed. "But we're still having problems getting the proper tools," he said. He held up one having a very distinct configuration. "I had to borrow this one off a buddy of mine. He's keeping my first-born male child until he gets it back."

Mills grinned. "You really should requisition that and anything else you need, as soon as possible. I'm authorizing Lt. Fridel and the others to make whatever purchases they need to in the next month."

"That'll help some, Captain," the Chief said, "but this ship's got a long way to go to get better."

"I understand that, Chief. That's why I appreciate those of you who are hard at it. Just hang in there and let me know where you need me to help."

"Sir," the Chief continued, "I'm not one to complain, but I am running low on chips. I've had my buddies fabricate parts in the machine shops of some of the tenders, in Norfolk and Philadelphia and even from the Coast Guard Yard. I have borrowed, begged, and finagled to get what I need. Now I'm down to actual requisitions."

"You have done well, for the *Card,* Senior Chief. Fill out the *actual* requisitions if you remember how."

"Oh, I have Williams for that Captain."

"You're in good hands, then Chief."

Thursday, 19 March 1970
USS Card Pier Side
US Coast Guard Base Curtis Bay, Maryland

1100: Lieutenant Grubaugh visited Lieutenant (j.g.) Cavatini. "I'm trying to get all my systems in condition for some bodacious exercise scenarios," Grubaugh explained. "Gallagher was willing to put up with a lot of 'touch-and-tell' simulation during weapons system exercises, but I don't think the new skipper is going to settle for half-measures like that. Do you remember when you first arrived aboard? I asked you about having your Electronics Technicians take a look at the Torpedo Launch Simulator?"

Mr. Cavatini nodded. "If I remember right, it was beyond their capability."

"Whom would they take it to on shore to get it back in operation?" The Lieutenant asked. "I'd like to get someone moving on it pretty soon."

The young lieutenant (jg) hesitated. "Are you sure this is a good idea? I'm not saying I'm not willing to help you, but remember the last time we tried something like this? My E-Lab put in some long over-time hours to get the air-search radar tuned and calibrated for an exercise Lieutenant Sterling was working on only to have us sit around for the next six months tied up to the pier. How much extra effort do we want to ask of these people without some assurance it'll be worth their while?"

"They haven't got anything better to do with their time, do they?" Grubaugh asked.

"I'm trying to get them all more serious about their training programs and their career progression handbooks. If I pull them off that to spend time on a system that'll never get used again, it doesn't look like I'm very serious about training."

The Lieutenant's look was very concerned. "Mike, I'm very serious about helping the new skipper pull this thing off. I think it's the only way we're ever going to get our people to take us seriously about anything."

"And you really think he's got a chance?"

Grubaugh shrugged. "I dunno. I hope so. And either way, we haven't got much to lose, do we?"

"That's what I said when Gallagher asked me to get the underwater communication system pumped up, and before that it was the HF radio system. My techs grumbled about all that extra work and I made them do it anyway. Now they keep reminding me of it every time I bring up a major repair or overhaul job."

The Lieutenant thought for a moment. "Tell you what, can you just find out for me who to work with on base? I'll run the simulator down myself on Monday."

Lieutenant Grubaugh's next visit was to the Combat Information Center (CIC) where she found Lieutenant Sterling, the officer with whom she shared a stateroom when on-board.

The CIC officer was checking over lists of documents with a chief. After an exchange of pleasantries they got down to the purpose of Lieutenant Grubaugh's visit.

"I thought we should coordinate on which weapon systems ought to be written into the first exercise when we get underway," she explained. "I want to focus my department's efforts on getting those one or two systems up to speed. We can work on the others in a more methodical fashion later on."

"I like the catapult loaded with rocks," responded Sterling. "It's just about *Card's* speed."

"Aw, come on, George. I'm serious. I want to get my plan of action set and in operation."

"Hey, I'm serious too, roomie. Anything more high-tech than that is beyond this crew's ability."

"You heard what the new skipper said," Grubaugh persisted. "He's deadly serious about getting the *Card* operational and combat-ready again."

"They shouldn't have sent a guy like Mills to this ship," Sterling shook her head. "This garbage barge is more suitable for Gilligan and the Skipper," she said referencing Gilligan's Island, a TV situation comedy popular from September 26, 1964, to September 4, 1967. Eventually they settled on a likely scenario, which would exercise a sampling of each officer's system.

Lieutenant Grubaugh's third stop was at Lieutenant Winthrop's stateroom where she found the Operations Officer working at the foldout desk. After a few words of explanation, Grubaugh began to detail some of her ideas.

"Georgia and I suggest a scenario where the air-search radar tracks a reconnaissance flight. The aircraft stays well out of range, but radios in our position. Next, sea-search picks up incoming torpedoes. We respond and knock them out with cluster hedgehogs. Her plotters get a fix on the launch vessel and we respond with a Harpoon torpedo. Can you work that into your schedule for the first exercise out at sea?"

Mister Winthrop looked disdainfully at Grubaugh. "Phil, what are you doing?"

"Just following Captain Mills' orders, Mister Winthrop."

Mr. Winthrop shook his head. "Get real, Phil. Mills has no idea what he's up against. He's getting everybody all agitated over nothing. Do what you need to do to make it look like you are going along with his plan but don't expect it come to anything. The sooner he gets to be more realistic about the *Card's* situation, the less anyone has to suffer for it later. Mills is a consultant not a Captain. He will soon get the picture and be gone just like the others who took the job."

1300: The Captain returned to the deck. He walked along checking for indications that work had been accomplished. There was some evidence that some work was being done, but not much. The "weeping rust" stains he'd noted when he first saw his ship were still intact. But now he also checked items he'd been noticing since his first few days.

The engineering chiefs had said dependence on shore-supplied facilities and services had resulted in deterioration of systems the *Card* used when operating on her own. This was also true on deck. The gear used for refueling at sea was speckled with rust, and the mating surfaces pitted with corrosion. He tried swinging the receiving arm out, but it moved only with great effort, and then with a protest of grating noises. The mechanisms for lowering the motor whale boat were also rusted to the point where it would be unwise to use them.

He noted that corrosion was so advanced around the edges of several of the water-tight doors that their ability to seal properly was in doubt. As he proceeded on down the Port side, he spotted Lieutenant Junior Grade (j.g.) Hooper standing by the forward port rail, gazing out at the channel.

"Good afternoon, Mister Hooper."

Mister Hooper's head jerked in surprise and he spun around to see Captain Mills.

"I'm glad I ran into you. I've been waiting to review the progress of your departmental assessment and the status of your work reports."

The j.g. stammered for a moment and then said, "I instructed the Deck Chief to handle that Captain."

"It wasn't the Deck Chief's responsibility, Mister Hooper," said the Captain, enunciating the word "responsibility" very clearly, "it was yours. Maybe it was partly my fault for not making that clear enough, but I'll correct that here and now."

Mills paused and let the reserve officer realize where this conversation was going. When he saw that Hooper was "all ears," he continued. "When I assign you to see that a task is accomplished, it becomes your responsibility to me to see that it gets done. You may delegate your authority to a boatswain's Mate", an able-bodied seaman or anyone else to do the actual task; but that doesn't remove your responsibility to see it done. Do you understand?"

"Yes Sir, I do. It's just that when I tell one of the men to do it, he should be responsible also."

"He is accountable to you, Mister Hooper, but that doesn't relieve you of your responsibility to me to see that it gets done, any more than my telling you to get it done, relieves me of my responsibility to ComResDesRon to see that this vessel gets seaworthy."

"ComResDesRon is responsible to his commander to have a certain number of ships ready for the exercise in July. Of those ships, he's to present so many Destroyers. He can't do it all himself, so he made me responsible for the *Card* and loaned me enough of his authority to get the job done.

In the same vein, I can't get all of the individual tasks on this ship accomplished by myself, so I gave you," he said, pointing his index finger at the Ensign's chest for emphasis, "responsibility for getting the deck in operational order. By assigning you to the position of Deck Officer, I loaned you a portion of my authority that will allow you to get the job done."

Mister Hooper still looked a bit confused, so Mills continued. "If you look in the SORM [Ship's Organizational Regulation Manual] it spells out what you can do and who works for you. Since the Captain signs off on that document, it's like my personal check, giving you some authority from my account." He smiled. "Do you have any more questions, Mr. Hooper?"

The j.g. shook his head. Captain Mills looked at him for a moment, and then continued. "Getting back to my original question," he said, "I want to know where you are on your departmental assessment."

"I was supposed to have an eight-man work crew start on the outside of the bridge today," Hooper replied. "Except only four of them showed up, and I think all four went over to the shipyard for supplies."

"That doesn't tell me anything about your over-all plan for the work on the ship."

"But that's why they were going to start outside the bridge, Sir," Hooper explained. "Start at the top and work their way down and aft."

Captain Mills repeated part of his conversation with Lt. Fridel, making sure Hooper understood the idea of separating areas into discrete work projects and spelling out the tasks and timelines for their accomplishment.

"Mister Hooper I want to see your first draft at 1500 this afternoon. We will meet each day at 1500 until I am satisfied with your plan.

That plan will be complete by Friday at 1500. Understand?"

"Aye, Aye Captain."

As with his earlier conversation, the Deck Officer asked no questions nor did he take any notes. The Captain walked back to the wardroom and Mr. Hooper went below to find Lt. Winthrop and seek his advice.

Mister Cavatini entered the wardroom. "You wanted to see me Captain?"

"Yes Mister Cavatini, have a seat. I have been looking over your assessment and I am confused. There seems to be a great many problems here that appear to have been discovered on your watch but the dates are before your time. Crypto down-time and repairs not made, classified massages received from the naval communication station on the base, instead of being received on board. There are gross security violations. None of your accounts or registered pubs are current. How could this have happened in just nine months? Was this the status when you relieved your predecessor?"

"All that you see here, Captain, was what I inherited from Lieutenant Pearson. I have made some great inroads in the correction process, but it is just too much."

"Why did you relieve as a custodian of this department until all these items were squared away?"

"Lieutenant Pearson was on his way to an advanced crypto school that was to start in two weeks, and he needed to get his family moved and said that to get all this squared away would delay his departure and he would miss the school start date."

"Mister Cavatini, according to your relieving report there were no discrepancies."

"I didn't think it was that detailed, Captain, and he said the Radiomen on board could take care of most of it. Then I find I have one regular First Class Radioman, who can handle radio central but he doesn't have crypto clearance. I have one Third Class reserve, two Second Class and three Seaman Radioman strikers. None of the reserves had ever seen most of this stuff. Pearson said it was just a matter of a few days, and then I find that the discrepancies he told me about was not half of what I discovered when I finally got to it."

He paused a moment, breathed a sigh, and continued.

"Not only that but he left me with the idea that my Radiomen could handle Radio Central. Only the first class can handle it but he can't be there all the time. Now they are so frustrated they are ready to give up. They say it is too much pressure from fleet communications, and the guys from Nav-Comm-Sta who are doing most of their work."

"Let this be a lesson to you Mister. Cavatini. Never sign off on a relief custodial document until you are certain everything is in order and will not come back to bite you."

"Yes Captain, believe me, I learned that lesson. I was snookered by that rat."

"I understand you were not the only one."

The Captain leaned forward to make sure his next point would not be missed. "You need to bring your Radiomen and Signalmen in to help you with this work. Go to NAVSTA and see what help they can give you. I need to see your management skills here."

"Aye Sir."

"Ok Lieutenant Cavatini, you gave me your assessment, now give me a plan. We will talk again in four days."

1400: Lieutenant Grubaugh entered the wardroom to add to her plan and assessment to the Gantt board. She found Captain Mills sitting in a side chair, reading the assessment and "Get Well" plan and the scenario for the Hull-Mounted torpedo Sonar guidance system. Grubaugh had finished drafting it out the evening before.

"I'm gratified to see how you've 'hit the ground running', Lieutenant Grubaugh. I did a walk-through of your torpedo storage magazine. It was immaculate.

I'd be happy to have it undergo an inspection any time at all." He tapped a finger on the file of papers he was holding. "I can see how it got that way too. This plan shows a lot of attention to detail. It's this kind of work that will get this ship's company moving along toward our readiness goals. Keep at it and if you need anything, let me know. I'll be around."

The weapons officer was obviously delighted.

"I'm only too glad to do it, Sir. Speaking for myself, I think it's high time we got moving in a positive direction." She paused, not wanting to sound too effusive but still feeling that the Captain would appreciate positive feedback. Mills was still looking at the document, so Grubaugh continued.

"Captain, a lot of us on this ship don't like being part of such a losing team. We know it's going to be a tough haul to get the *Card* in shape to make an appearance at GITMO this year, but at least we're glad to have the real opportunity to try."

"Thank you, Lieutenant Grubaugh," the Captain answered looking up at the young officer, "I appreciate you saying that." Lieutenant Grubaugh continued, "I'm not going to make any excuses for the condition of any part of this ship, and that includes my own areas of responsibility. It's just that you should know that I and some of the officers stand behind you a hundred percent, and we'll do what we have to do to help you pull it off."

The Captain smiled again in appreciation, "I was quite sure just from looking at these documents you've been putting together that I would be able to count on you, Lieutenant."

"Thank you, Sir," the Lieutenant replied, then hesitated, trying to ease into the next topic.

"Sir, at the risk of speaking out of line, I want the Captain to know that there are -- well -- things happening on this ship that he needs to be aware of." Grubaugh looked for words, "he needs to watch out for -- well -- certain people in particular."

Mills looked intently at Grubaugh. "I think I catch your drift, Lieutenant. I appreciate what you're trying to do, but I think you'd be well advised to let it go at that."

"I understand, Captain," the Lieutenant nodded.

Ship Captains, and corporate executives, like straight answers, and straight talk and they value those who give it. The old adage "Bad News is better than no News" is a true one. While no one likes to hear bad news or straight answers that are not complimentary, the wise executive goes there first. In this case, Lieutenant Grubaugh could only tell him what he already knew, and if she had continued, she may think about it later and decide the Captain would construe this as *kissing up*, in which case she would feel vulnerable at their next meeting.

Captain Mills' last visit for the day was to that of Ensign Marshall Goldsmith.

He had dropped by several times earlier in the day but the Ensign had not been there. The Captain later noted that Ensign Goldsmith had been engaged in helping his men load and store supplies that had arrived on the pier in a truck at ten hundred.

1815: The 1-MC came alive with the sound of the duty Quartermaster's voice: "Now sweepers, sweepers man your brooms. Make a clean sweep down fore and aft. Sweep down all lower decks ladders and passageways. Empty all trashcans. Lay below to the MAA office for muster, all restricted persons."

1830: The click of the on-off switch of the 1-MC sent a metallic tone through the intercom system. It was a sound, seasoned Navy sailors come to notice readily. The sound was followed by the booming voice of the duty Boatswain's Mate; "Now attention to colors." The entire ship's company stopped what they were doing and waited in silence. Those on the outside weather decks stopped, faced the Ensign and brought up a right hand salute. They remained that way until the "Carry On" signal was called.

2000: Eight O'clock reports were piped over the 1-MC. It was twenty hundred (8:00 PM) when Goldsmith reported to the Captain's cabin. "I think the Captain will be quite pleased with the condition of my division," began Ensign Goldsmith after he was seated at the table. "We're running a completely non-automated accounting system on this ship, but the fleet audit of our books got the highest rating."

"That's very commendable," replied Captain Mills. "I also noted that your bi-weekly updates have been uniformly complete, on time and that they balance to the penny. And in personnel, the leave accounting system and personnel files are also in excellent shape." The Ensign looked grateful for the compliment.

"However," the Captain continued, "You've still got some areas that need to be worked."

"I know that, Sir, no one else on this ship has the variety of responsibilities I have. Besides everything in supply, finance and personnel, I have all the food storage and service, including the dining areas. Then there's the ship's store, barbershop, and laundry. It's an awful lot to keep up with."

"I understand that, but that's why you can't afford to develop 'tunnel vision'. You're doing an exceptional job in some areas but have a lot of holes in others. You're going to have to develop more of a manager's perspective on your areas of responsibility. That means not doing your people's work for them, and not just working your in-basket."

"Does that mean the Captain would be willing to settle for lower ratings on the audits?" The officer asked, a bit pointedly.

"Not at all Mister Goldsmith, but I would certainly like to see you pass what you know about posting and checking accounts on to your enlisted people. I can't think of a better situation than to have six Marshall Goldsmiths on my ship."

The Ensign was flattered, but unsure of himself now. "I'm not sure it's something you can teach people. I just have to spend a lot of time on them."

"I understand that very well. But that's all the more reason for you to let your people do their own work. I've watched people try to type with one finger. That one finger goes like the dickens and wears itself out while the rest of them just stay motionless and get out of shape."

"But they're not sitting around getting out of shape," Goldsmith protested. "They've been unloading stores and putting them below decks since ten hundred this morning."

"Your people should not need to do that by themselves. When you're expecting a re-supply, you request assistance from every other department on this ship. If the job takes longer than three hours, you're not getting the support you should have."

Mister Goldsmith looked subdued. "With all due respect, Captain, I don't think you understand how things are on this ship."

Captain Mills leveled his gaze back at the Ensign. "How things *were* on this ship, Mister Goldsmith," he said distinctly. "They're not going to be that way anymore." The discussion continued Captain Mills presented a number of items he'd noted during his visits around the ship. The Ensign left the cabin with five pages of notes.

Captain Mills stopped by Mister Winthrop's stateroom to ask about the status of the requisitions. He had not yet secured them. Mister Winthrop assured him they would be on his desk by noon tomorrow.

Friday, 20 March 1970
USS Card - Pier Side
US Coast Guard Yard, Curtis Bay Maryland

0700: Lt Sterling met with the Captain in the Wardroom. The Captain had a ten-hundred meeting at the Navy Base but he needed to speak with Sterling and get her report. He read her report with keen attention. He made some notes in selected sections. Finally, he closed the report and pushed it across the table toward her.

He leaned back in his chair. "You have done a remarkable job with what you have to work with. There is no money in the budget for an upgrade, but we must interface with the other ships in the squadron and with GITMO. Can we do that with this level of technology?"

"I'm not sure Captain," she answered.

"You have a First Class Radarman, who has just come from GITMO...."

"Jawarski."

"Jawarski. Work with Jawarski on this. The flag is on the *Rogers*. Check with CIC on the *Rogers*. Go visit them if you have to. Make the changes I noted in here and give me a realistic assessment of our Interface capabilities. When will you have this?"

She consulted her wristwatch. "Forty-eight hours Captain."

"Keep in touch."

Chapter 4 - Executive Assessment General Quarters - Battle Stations

Leadership, management and command

The Captain has provided sufficient time for his subordinate managers to show some operational improvement and they have failed to produce. Department heads must know the condition of the organization under their custody and have effective methods for continuous assessment and plans for maintaining its performance.

When we assess the management team it appears that Lt. Winthrop has the upper hand. But let's look at the realities of the management situation. This is a good time to assess the captain's Leadership, Management and Command.

Leadership

Leadership is the ability to influence the behavior and thinking of others. Leaders are visionaries, motivators, and providers of resources. Power is the essence of leadership. It is the *"clout" one has in professional and personal relationships.*

When we talk about leadership a myriad of meanings come to mind. It seems that every one has an idea of what leadership is, but I have heard few definitions that I think actually define leadership. We know it when we see it. We know when it is lacking in an organization.

General Dwight D. Eisenhower said leadership is "Getting other people to do what you want them to do, when you want them to do it, the way you want them to do it, because they want to do it" *(1943)*. That in a nutshell is leadership. Now let's examine the person engaged in leadership; the leader.

Leaders are the true minority in this world. If there ever was a minority group leadership is the defining factor. There are few leaders in this world. They are few who are willing to shoulder the awesome burden of guiding others to the accomplishment of a worthwhile objective. What makes leaders unique?

They like seeing their plans reach fruition. *Most of the world does not have plans.*

They are willing to make decisions that affect themselves and others and assume the consequences for those decisions. *Most of the world cannot make decisions that affect others or assume the consequences.* They are willing to take the responsibility for their own performance and the performance of others. *Most of the world is made up of those who are not willing to take the responsibility for their own performance.*

Leaders are the energy that turns the gears of industry and government. Without leaders there would be no organization, no structure, and no productivity. There would be chaos, confusion, frustration, and stagnation. Independent talent, skills and resources will not accomplish much unless they are focused on a worthwhile task.

You may have seen many articles regarding the qualities of a leader and the perquisites to leadership. You can recite the Boy Scout oath and call those qualities of leadership.

But noble qualities do not define the leader. Hitler had few noble qualities, if any, yet that he was a true leader is undisputed.

In the past 23 years I have come to know many fine leaders each having unique qualities that have served them in their leadership roles. I have found 4 perquisites that are common in all of them.

1. A Strong Sense of Self.

Leadership is influencing the behavior and thinking of others. Leaders influence others by giving them a sense of security when those others believe, that the leaders believe in themselves. A leader requires a strong, appropriate self-image.

2. A strong Sense of Mission.

The success or failure of an organization depends substantially upon the success with which its leaders move their teams toward meeting organizational goals.

This requires the leader to understand the purpose of the organization, why the organization exists, and the part their department, section, or unit plays in the overall scheme of things. The leader is the power that focuses the individual energies of the members of the group toward the accomplishment of the organization's mission. It includes providing direction, encouragement, instruction, refreshment, resources and training.

3. A sense of stewardship.

The leader is a steward of the organization's resources; the natural custodian of its mission, its future, its stability, its reputation and its methods. Stewardship is firmly planted in the leader's philosophy and personal integrity. The leader's word must be accountable; others must be able to depend on it. The very fact that one is followed means their integrity can be trusted. People entrust their careers, their futures and sometimes their lives, their physical and mental health to the leader.

4. A keen sense of Followership.

Followership has two sides: *The leader as a subordinate to a higher authority and the leader as an influencer of those who follow.* The leader must recognize that they are subordinate to a higher authority and must conduct themselves toward this higher authority, as they would expect their followers to conduct themselves. The leader is a role model to others. The most valuable people, in the organization are those who whole-heartedly carry out their boss' objectives.

The leader of those who follow must be ever mindful that regardless of how astute the leader may be that leader must realize the importance of those in the ranks. No one alone can bring about the success of an organization, without loyalty to the crew, vision, generosity and competence, as demonstrated toward the crew.

In order to be a leader, a man must have followers. To have followers, a man must have their confidence. Hence the supreme quality for a leader is unquestionably integrity.

Without it, no real success is possible, no matter whether it is on a section gang, a football field, in an army, or in an office. If a man's associates find him guilty of phoniness, if they find that he lacks forthright integrity, he will fail. His teachings and actions must square with each other. The first great need, therefore, is integrity and high purpose (Dwight D. Eisenhower 1944).

Management

Management is the judicious use of authority, agency power and politics for the purpose of accomplishing a worthwhile objective for the benefit of an organization. We introduced the concept of management in chapter one, so it will suffice to just remind us of what we said. Management is orchestrating independent competencies toward a worthwhile objective so a desired outcome can be realized. Management is the executive function of planning, organizing, directing, coordinating and controlling.

The chief executive is there to ensure the organization operates for the purpose for which it was organized. We talked about tight and loose control methods of management, and we said that Captain Gallagher exercised abdication management. Abdication is not loose control it is abandoning the command structure and the stewardship of the organization and its mission. The opposite end of the management spectrum is worse; micro management.

I was called in to do an organizational assessment of a privately owned corporation under the command of the founder's son. It was a midsize manufacturing operation that employed about 750 people.

The company's operation included sales, marketing, R&D, manufacturing and distribution from the same facility. Productivity and sales had taken a nose dive nine months ago and showed no signs of improving, even though no major changes had occurred in the industry or the way the company did business.

I interviewed every member of the management team, and a stratified sampling of employees in each department. I looked at samples of production reports, reports from Q.C, sales, R&D and maintenance. I looked at certain items the controller was tracking for monthly and quarterly reports.

What I discovered was the president made an incredible acquisition thirteen months prior to my assignment in order to increase the company's market share. He recruited the top sales manager, production manager, plant manager, engineer, and QC and R&D managers from competitors by offering them considerably more money, and the opportunity to work for a well respected and growing organization.

He had the top hands in the industry focusing their time and talent on his business, but they could not make a decision or carry out a plan without his approval.

He inadvertently thwarted their efforts and had frozen their desire to contribute to the organization's mission." I suggested he visit another of his plants far away and leave this one alone for six months.

Establish a challenging goal for each of his executive team members, call in each Friday at 11 AM, cater lunch and have them report their plans, their activities and their progress. He did and his company came back to life.

In an interview coach Bear Bryant was reminded that he was noted for hiring coaches that were smarter than he, and they were strong willed coaches. Coach Bryant responded by saying "Well it's true, I want coaches that are smarter than I am, or at least as smart as I am, I want coaches that know football and can carry out my plan. The interviewer then asked; "You are a strong willed person yourself, how does that work, strength against strength?"

"Its not strength against strength, said the bear, I'm the boss! I listen to them and I incorporate things they say into the plan if it's the right thing to do at the time, but when they walk away they go to carry out my plan, my orders, they do it my way, because I am ultimately responsible. Whether it works out well or not, it is my responsibility.

The Captain did not believe Lieutenant Winthrop when he said the pubs were up to date. Either the Captain already knew the answer or he suspected the Lieutenant was not paying attention and had not ordered their updates and once again he was caught unprepared. If the junior officer was paying attention to his job he would have caught on to the fact that the Captain knows what the OIC is required to do, and get it done before the captain asks about it. Something as germane to the "Get Well Plan" as Navy Regulations needed attention and Lieutenant Winthrop was the responsible party.

Registered publications are those official rules, regulations, best practices and legal initiatives that provide management with the guidance in order to remain in a legal standing or to stay on top of current trends in the field. An important aspect in operations control is having current industry and organizational information.

Mr. Winthrop's answer to the captain's question was a clear indication of the extent of Mr. Winthrop's lack of control. The captain will make a note of Mr. Winthrop's answer and devise a plan to allow Mr. Winthrop to discover the importance of the inquiry, and get the publications up to date.

But this incident is not enough. The captain must exert his authority and power, or the Winthrop mindset will continue to prevail in the management ranks and we have seen what his management style has done to the ship and the crew. When a subordinate manager is actively opposing the senior executive, the senior must be active not passive. Authority must be exercised to be accepted.

Of course the captain could fire Mr. Winthrop and make an example of him. Even though he was treading dangerously close to insubordination, the captain's plan for Mister Winthrop was to convert him.

It will take persistence, will power and exposing his immaturity and inexperience believing this to be a more powerful lesson than eliminating him. The captain must confront him - challenge him, not coddle him.

He must get the subordinate's mind off himself and onto some worthy objective. This is the time when the senior executive should assign the subordinate manager to a project that will totally occupy his time, and mental energy. It must be an assignment with monumental consequence, a success or failure assignment that will make a significant impact on the organization's operation. He must be held accountable for each segment in the operation. The assignment must offer him the opportunity to achieve or fail and suffer personal consequences of either. We want him to succeed.

Stewardship

Management and stewardship are synonymous; but all too often the stewardship aspect of management is lost in the daily PODCC *(planning, organizing, directing, coordinating and controlling)*. Both are identified as the act of managing or supervising the property, budget and affairs of a principal. In short, stewardship and management is having the custody of another's prosperity and well being. But stewardship goes further into the responsibility segment of management. Stewardship refers to the personal attention a manager gives to every aspect of the principal's affairs and well-being. Not just the daily operation of the entity but to those employed by it. Executives are the stewards of the organization's resources, the natural custodian of its stability, its future, its reputation, its methods, its vision and values. The chief executive is the chief Steward. Stewardship is the primary requisite to command.

Command

Although seen by some as being military, or militaristic and totally authoritarian such gross characterization of command is not valid and has never been valid. When management commissions managers and assigns them responsibility for the mission of the organization a legitimate command is established.

That legitimate command provides a legal basis for the exercise of the broad activities of leadership and management directed toward the accomplishment of a worthwhile Mission for the benefit of the organization.

Actually command encapsulates five aspects of operational management; the first aspect refers to the **mandate,** or specific mission of the organization that is purposely assembled to initiate action directed toward carrying out specific activities for which it was designed.

Command is the lawful, **legitimate authority** which an individual exercises over subordinates by virtue of the assignment. Command is control. Next is the operational and management **structure** of an organization, the way it is designed to meet the demands of the organization's purpose and those in the organization who carry out the activities that achieve that purpose.

The command consists of all resources needed to do the job including people, materials, tools, equipment, money and assigned duties for each. Command is the amalgamation of management and leadership by virtue of **Executive Decisions**.

The one in command must be one who has demonstrated certain ability for situational analysis, who can take all the information make sense of it, and impose order to it.

The one in command is the one who must make certain that each part matches the whole, the one who must decide to take the responsibility and act.

Those who raise to the top of their chosen careers share a common characteristic: They are decisive. They make decisions. They take risks. Managers in command positions reduce that risk, and make decisions by drawing on their own experiences. Commanders learn to learn from their own experiences and the experiences of others. They develop the ability to draw conclusions from past events and accumulated information over their managerial lifetime. They learn to develop their own "Rules of Command", or "Rules of Thumb", or "Management axioms." Whatever they call them. They establish a philosophy or personal protocol, or programmed decisions, that say when this situation presents itself this action has usually proven to be the best approach. They step up and choose a course of action and go with it.

Decisions are always made under conditions of uncertainty.

We make decisions or best guesses using what information we have available at the time with all the intelligence and discernment at our disposal and hope for the best. There will be consequences if you act. There are consequences if you don't act. There will be consequences regardless of the decision you make, but you accept the consequences and make adjustments are necessary to make the best use of those consequences.

Incomplete knowledge is not the same as ignorance. Informed judgments can still be made, indeed they must be made

Any time a decision is needed to change, start up, create or discontinue a course of action, an unknown situation is created which involves a risk.

The one in command is the one who is in charge and has the elements of control firmly in hand. To be in command is to be in command of the command. Again quoting Captain Mills;" Everyone who is assigned to a management position brings to that job their own philosophy of command. That philosophy is the sum total of everything one has read, seen, heard or thought. We read textbooks on leadership, we've sat through lectures and seminars on command, watched our superiors succeed or fail by their actions, and had our own attempts turn out well or poorly. Through all these experiences, we've each developed our own thoughts and ideas concerning the proper way to command an organization.

Command is **custody or stewardship.** Most of all it is custody of the organization. Command competence includes much more than exercise of leadership or management techniques. The one in command is the ultimate point of responsibility for the organization.

That one in command is the protector the one responsible for the safe keeping its operation, its stability, its future the guardianship of its mission, its reputation, its resources and all who are employed in it. While authority can be delegated command responsibility and accountability remains with the executive in charge (Commander).

The captain identified the custodial aspect of command in a meeting with Mr. Winthrop. "Mr. Winthrop, my responsibility for this ship is not diminished when you assume O.I.C. duties. I am still accountable for it. I'm responsible every hour of the day. I am responsible for the condition of this ship, the daily production, the conduct of the crew and for the quality of the training that goes on. That responsibility is in effect at all times."

Mister McCormick, in one of his missions to get the Captain to abandon his plans for the ship, suggested that Captain Mills share leadership with Mr. Winthrop, as Captain Gallagher did. The Captain's response was worthy of a management axiom.

He said "I believe in sharing leadership Mr. McCormick. I don't believe in sharing command. There can only be one skipper. Captain Gallagher shared command and you see where that got you. Believe me Mr. McCormick I will expect you and Mr. Winthrop to assume your share of leadership."

Power, Authority & Politics

The senior manager's performance is measured by the ability to accomplish tasks through the efforts of others. These others are subordinates, peers, seniors and anyone you can persuade both inside and outside the organization. There are three necessary elements that must be present if the exercise of leadership; management and command are to be effective. Those elements are; power, authority and politics. The effective executive exercises leadership through the appropriate use of power and management through the judicial employment of authority and politics.

Power, authority, and politics have gotten a lot of bad press over the years. Hard feelings and negative prejudices have demonized the words because of the various definitions that have been placed on them. The fact is that power, authority and politics are neither *moral* nor *immoral*. They are *amoral*. They are not intended to be abusive like Hitler, Stalin and Attila the *Hun. When exercised appropriately, power, authority and politics will bring order and predictable results to any organized activity.

Power itself may have the worst reputation. The term provokes strong but mixed emotions. Some have had uncomfortable or demoralizing experiences because of the abuse of another's power.

Some appreciate what power can do and accept it as an institutional norm. The traditional image of the powerful as arrogant, demanding and of the powerless as fearful and ingratiating is a false one. But power is a useful medium if properly secured and exercised.

Abusive power is destructive to everyone, including the one abusing it. But it is *powerlessness*, not power, that undermines organizational effectiveness.

Power is ability to influence the behavior and thinking of others by virtue of a person's persona or by virtue of the position they hold. It is the authentic right of the leader to make certain types of requests, to give orders and to direct the activities of others. The organization appoints a person to a position, and with that appointment is the legitimate power in which one can have an effect on the plans and activities of others. If one is unable to have an effect on the plans and activities of those with whom he or she interacts, the others have more power.

*There is some evidence that Attila was good to his people but a terror to those with whom he did battle.

If one can affect the plans and activities of others and others have the same effect, power is equal. If one can affect the plans and activities of others and they cannot have an effect in return, then one has the greater power.

The job parameters will allow for non-ordinary action, a show of discretion, the exercise of judgment, and innovative risk-taking activities without having to go through others for approval. Those with legitimate power have the backing of other important people in the organization whose tacit approval becomes another resource.

There are in effect two kinds of power: personal power and Agency power.

Agency Power

Agency Power is position power. It is the ability to influence the behavior and thinking of others through the authority to influence careers and agency comfort. *Agency power adheres in positions, not in the person holding the position.* Regardless of how cordial the feelings are between you and your subordinates, employees defer to the will of the boss. They do it because the executive has authority over them; the unspoken recognition of that authority is significant.

Agency power comes with the trappings of management provided by the organization. These trappings are evidence that the organization has entrusted and bequeathed a person with the right to use authority and agency power.

In the military those trappings include special rank insignias, special uniform markings, a required salute by subordinates, and certain privileges. In civilian life executives have an office, administrative help, name on the door and an impressive title. Recognized agency power is also demonstrated by the degree of freedom that can be exercised by the executive.

The evidence of legitimate power means that one has effective lines in a formal framework.

The measure of agency legitimate power is demonstrated by the extent to which the manager has access to and authority over *lines of supply, lines of information and lines of support.*

Lines of supply refer to the manager's capacity to bring in the things that his or her organization needs: materials, money, rewards, and the ability to distribute resources and perhaps even prestige.

Lines of information refer to the capacity of the manager to gain access to important information in time to take action. It is being in-the-know from formal and informal sources.

Lines of support refers to the influence one has with others who are willing to offer support for the manager's ideas and decisions—support from superiors, peers and subordinates. The most necessary support is from seniors. It must be understood that while legitimate power is provided by the commission, which requires subordinate others to obey, those subordinate others may choose to ignore or circumvent this power. This has an effect of reducing the effectiveness of the legitimate power, and perhaps results in the removal of this legitimate power by the organization's authorities. To some especially the officers and crew of the Card, it may appear the Captain had very little power. Does he have lines of supply?

In spite of the fact that Winthrop sat on requisitions, the captain has power of the supply line. Mr. Winthrop could not have gotten away much longer before someone got curious. Perhaps Yeoman Williams would have spotted the delay and notified the captain, but certainly NavBase and ComResDesRon would check into it.

Does he have lines of information? He does. He has access to ComResDesRon and NavBase and those enlisted and officers on the Card who keep him informed. Does he have lines of support? He does, ComResDesRon has given him a mission to bring the Card up to combat readiness.

The captain can be assured of their support. He has the support of Grubaugh, Sterling, and Cavatini. These officers may not be in the clique with McCormick, Winthrop, Fridel, Hooper and Winchester, but their competence and self reliance gives them the personal power and political connections with important enlisted personnel to be a worthy ally and support for the captain.

Over-reliance on position power can have negative consequences.

Personal Power

Personal Power is the ability to influence the behavior and thinking of others based on individual characteristics such as personal philosophy, integrity, self reliance, demeanor, intelligence and behavior. Personal power adheres in people, not in positions. Personal power is present without the trappings of rank or position. It is reference power that causes others to react without giving or promising tangible rewards or punishments.

Personal power comes from purpose and conviction—an indomitable will to carry through in difficult times. Leaders with personal power display a "can-do" attitude that becomes a source of strength for their people and stimulates in them a strong sense of purpose.

Perhaps the greatest characteristic that contributes to one's having personal power is the appearance of having one's life in order—the appearance of being comfortable with one's self.

Personal power is based on the belief that it is in the best interest of others to pay attention to the one having this power, and to follow their lead.

Others are willing to allow one with personal power to influence their behavior and thinking because of the competence and skill they display confidence in the judgment of the power. Knowledge power is not only achieved by what one knows, but also, **who** one knows.

Persistence is yet another trait of personal power. There are those who think that persistence and politicking will bring them to the levels of success for which they are striving. But persistence, without talent, or intelligence will only deliver one to their highest level of incompetence.

Probably the most noticeable attribute of personal power is the clear presence of intelligence. Exhibited by displaying a grasp or understanding of what is going on. Intelligence is displayed in a number of ways; another is the obvious effective form of power that is derived through the use of appropriate and mature behavior. Behavior power begins with "bearing" or "court presence," which strikes instantly, before anyone even knows if the person holds agency power or rank.

Webster's *New World Dictionary* defines *bearing* as "*the manner in which a person carries and conducts themselves. Deportment is physical posture, self control, facial expression, conduct and demeanor. Deportment is a distinctive air, appearance, or presence. It is the quality of commanding respectful attention, an attitude of expectancy and the appearance of a positive image.*"

Then there is personal credibility and reputation. The degree to which the manager is esteemed by the manager's boss and others in authority affects the scope of authority. Believing they are under the command of a competent and mature leader makes subordinates feel more worthy.

To ensure victory the troops must have confidence in themselves as well as their managers; this cannot be attained unless the troops believe the manager is worthy.

Alexander the Great never lost a battle. Even though he lost men in a battle, he never lost a battle in the 15 years he spent conquering the world. He did not lose a battle because his men thought they were invincible because Alexander was their commander.

Authority:

Authority is absolutely essential to get things done, but it can't be put into a job description. Authority is to the organizational world what gravity is to the physical world. It orders the relationships between people so they can co-exist harmoniously and work together effectively.

No society, or any part of society, can exist without a system of structure and authority. The absence of authority is anarchy. Managerial authority gives the manager the means by which he or she can create and maintain an environment of performance. Authority is the expressed right to command, to give orders and to secure resources, to determine, what they are, how and when they will be used and by whom. Those resources include money, material, personnel, and assistance from others.

It is important to note here, that the manager must accept and exercise authority. Most failed management promotions are caused by the newly appointed manager's refusal to accept and employ it. Subordinates expect it. The Manager's commission grants authority. A person with personal power translates and communicates his or her ability to influence the behavior of others through the proper exercise of legitimate authority. The organization's management commissions these people to use that personal power for the organization's benefit. This commission provides authority and agency power to assist the leader in the attainment of commissioned responsibilities.

Organizational authority, like agency power adheres in positions and not in people. Without the ability to influence the behavior of others, the executive's authority erodes to illegitimacy. Authority within an organization is influenced by the behavior and attitudes of the workers within that organization. If they accept the values, policies and procedures set forth by the organization, and if they believe in the organization's vision and values, they are more likely to cooperate with formal authority.

In some cases workers will form informal groups and temporarily appoint their own authority in contrast to formal authority. Case in point, Mr. McCormick outranked Mr. Winthrop, but the crew recognized Mr. Winthrop, effectively edging the duly appointed authority.

Management Axiom: Authority is a sacred trust—one that should not be abused.

Politics:

The manager's job requires getting things done by utilizing resources and working with others. Getting things done through others means any others who can move resources and deliver results. More often than not, that function is directly related to the political position of those who initiate the action. Organizational politics are the tactics used to increase one's personal or agency power, or to have access to resources not under the leader's authority.

Politics are an important aspect of managerial leadership in any organized activity because of the interdependence inherent in the organization.

Managers are affected by situations in which they have little control and by people who don't report to them: suppliers, customers, political groups, etc. Power depends on influence. Politics are actions taken to put oneself in a position to influence those with access to resources and situations and use them for the benefit of the manager, the group, and the organization.

The old adage "It's not what you know, it's who you know" is not completely without merit. Many decisions are made with political considerations. Executives are promoted to positions of responsibility because they know how to get things done and they know who to go to for additional support. There is no doubt about it: the most influential and effective people are those with an active Rolodex, a network, and a contact list. They know whom to call, and they have access to those people. Effective leaders establish and maintain relationships with influential people and maintain a network of people who have access to resources and influence over others.

Political alliances are not made by bootlicking or running a continuous popularity poll. They are established through credible work and personal relationships assisted by smooth running of a competent operation. Politics is networking, getting out and circulating about the complex. Meet people, talk to people. If you run a staff service department it means getting out there and selling that service. It means getting support for new programs; it means sharing information. Appropriate use of political influence carries great clout. If you run a line operation networking is building a network of colleagues that will support your legislation through the executive legislative process.

This is association power. Political power influences others because they believe this person has influence over other powerful people who could influence their lives and careers. One who is connected with others who have authority or power is sought out by others who want to be counted among those who know the power.
There is a perception that one who has many allies can marshal forces or rally influential others to assist in some campaign or secure resources for themselves or others.

Subordinates especially take pride in their leaders and want them to have status or "clout" with others, especially those in high places. The more political clout one has and the greater the status their leaders have, the better they feel about themselves.

Politics are an integral part of the agency power element of management. But political agency power can corrupt one who does not also possess a strong self-power.

The strain to gain agency power, when it is not earned is the number one factor to "one-ups-man-ship politics. Political in-fighting where managers play games to attain prominence is hurtful to the organizational and everyone connected to it, as all organizational resources are considered to be expendable for personal political gain.

"One-ups-man-ship" political tactics are not very effective over the long run. Securing political support for selfish motives will eventually backfire.

Among the unethical forms of politics are discrediting others so that one looks good in comparison setting up a rival to fail, hiding important information from coworkers so they will perform poorly giving insincere compliments to powerful people to gain their short term approval.

And don't be fooled by thinking politics is keeping on the good side of high level people. There is a group of people I call "*Rumpelstilskins*." You may recall a fairy tale from the Brothers Grimm about an obscure dwarf that could spin gold out of straw. Rumpelstilskins are usually very competent key people, not usually out in front. They may be unofficial leaders or they just may be a clerk or an administrative type that has access to useful information, or resources. Many times they have limited signature or decision authority from the power to whom they report. Because of their competence and initiative they not only have access to those who have power and authority, they have the respect of their boss, higher ups and peers.

They are central to the flow of information and ideas. Information and ideas are brought to them by those who hope to exchange worthwhile data for other worthwhile data. An effective manager discovers these Rumpelstilskins and finds out how they like their coffee, when they celebrate their birthday . . . and . . . well you get the idea. You do favors for them, and they do the same for you. They can save you time, and frustration. These people are sent for special training, and are granted opportunities to exercise judgment in the use of that training. The smart executive not only finds the Rumpelstilskins and uses them, they are careful to hire those who are of this ilk and place them in visible administrative roles.

You will recall from chapter one, the Captain made a powerful political alliance with Yeoman First Class Petty Officer Williams. Williams is a pivot point in the organization. He has political connections to all the competent people on board the ship, and in NavBase, the Bureau of Personnel, Guantanamo Bay testing personnel, and who knows where else. And now, he has the "gate" to the captain.

Management Axiom:
Ship captains like straight answers, and straight talk and they value those who give it. The old adage "Bad news is better than no news" is a true one. While no one likes to hear bad news or straight answers that are not complimentary, the wise executive goes there first.

You do not need to do the uncommon. You only need to do the common uncommonly well.

It must be understood that while legitimate power is provided by the commission, which requires subordinate others to obey, those subordinate others may choose to ignore or circumvent this power.

This has an effect of reducing the effectiveness of the legitimate power, and perhaps results in the removal of this legitimate power by the organization's authorities. Probably the most effective form of power is derived through the use of appropriate and mature behavior. Behavior power begins with "bearing" or "court presence," which strikes instantly, before anyone even knows if the person holds agency power or rank.

Chapter 5
Battle Condition X-Ray

Friday, 20 March 1970

**US Naval Support Facility,
Potomac River, WASHDC
Reserve Destroyer Division 5 Command**

Captain Mills drove out to the Navy base to make the rounds and maintain his political alliances with the "brass." He was scheduled to meet with Buck Sorenson at 1300, but a phone call from his boss' Chief of Staff informed him that Captain Sorenson was called to Philadelphia and would not be able to meet him. He said Captain Mills would meet with Admiral Pulaski, ComResDesDiv himself.

Mill's first stop was the Expediting Department at the Navy Supply Center. He had told the person who had answered the telephone earlier that day that he wanted to make his visit in person. Mills was escorted to the second-floor office of Commander Preston Simmons.

Commander Simmons stood up when Mills entered the room. "Bob, how delightful to see you again It's been a long time! So what can I help you with?"

"I wanted to stop by and renew an old acquaintance," Mills began. "As you know, I'm the new skipper on the *Card,* and I've got the task of getting her back into shipshape and ready to join the squadron in Jacksonville in July. We're going to need all the help we can get, for equipment items as well as for supplies and materiel. I didn't want to insult you by just loading your people up with paper and not coming by to re-introduce myself to you first."

"Well, I appreciate the thought, Bob" smiled Simmons, leaning back in his swivel chair, "But I thought you were well on top of it all with that sharp OIC you've got there on *Card*. I got a message from him this past week about all the inspections he's had the ship's officers performing, all the needs for repairs and updated equipment they'll be sending through my department soon, and generally making it sound that they're doing their toughest work for you." The Commander grinned, "The way it sounded to me, Bob, was that you were one lucky guy in the draw and could just sit back and wait for fortune and fame to start rolling in."

"Well we both know you can't get complacent," Mills said with a fairly convincing smile. "The moment you let down your guard is the time you get bitten by whatever it was that got overlooked."

"Yeah," the other agreed, "You've got a point there. Still in all, I'd have to say it sounds like you've got a darn good team pulling for you."
Captain Mills changed the subject then, and began to work out details with Commander Simmons for getting contract technicians assigned to the *Card's* propulsion plant as well as the power generation system.

Mills left the building and drove to the headquarters of ComResDesDiv5. Before meeting with the Admiral he was scheduled to meet with another old acquaintance, Commander Mike Marshall. This meeting was even more disquieting than had been the news from Simmons.

"For a while there, Bob, requisitions from your ship were coming in fast and accurate, and I was impressed with how quickly you got a handle on things. Then those requisitions just stopped. Then they began to trickle in slowly with a lot of errors. I was curious so I took a look at them and the first ones were signed by First Class Yeoman Williams, and the bad ones are now being signed by Ensign Marshall Goldsmith. I got a feelin' your Yeoman had been outflanked. Your Yeoman Williams does not pass bad paper, and Mr. Goldsmith can tell you the serial numbers on the dollar bills in his pocket."

"I'll look into it Mike."

"Don't bother. My Yeoman called the supply Yeoman, who called your Yeoman. They took care of it. I'm afraid you got a shark in your locker. Frankly, Bob, this Winthrop guy you've got as OIC is a snake in the grass," Marshall declared. "The word around headquarters now is that he's been working like mad to get the ship ready for sea. He claims he's got a stack of requisitions for equipment and repair services just waiting to put in the system, but 'his Captain' is just sitting on them."

The *Card's* Captain tightened his lip and slowly shook his head from side to side.

"The impression around this building is that the upgrading of the ship and its crew is being done through the initiative of one Lieutenant John D. Winthrop III, Officer in CHARGE of the *USS Card,* grandson of Winston D. Winthrop himself and favorite nephew of Rear Admiral Dunhill Winthrop. The bottom line on that, buddy boy, is that you ought to take the advice of the jet jockeys at NavAir and keep an eye on your six o'clock." He motioned behind himself with his thumb.

Mills' mouth was drawn into a tight-lipped line before he spoke.

"ComResDesRon told me I would be sailing into a red sunrise (reference to red sky in the morning, sailor take warning), but I can't spend my whole time looking in the rear view mirror, Mike. I appreciate your Intel, and I will be wary about handing anyone an opening for a cheap shot, but the more I look back, the less I look forward. The next thing you know, the forecasts of doom become a self-fulfilling prophecy. I've got to stay my course and not get distracted by the sideshows. I'm responsible for the whole ship and the whole crew, not just Bob Mills."

Marshall nodded; then with a grin he added, "Say, do you remember how ole' Elvis-Preston described that Exec back on the *Ed Mitchell?*" He said, 'The guy was down on his hands and knees looking for piss-ants and the elephants came running across the deck and stomped him to death."

Captain Mills bit his lip but smiled, then said, "Well, I don't put Winthrop in the same category as a piss-ant, but he's no elephant either."

"As I said before, Bob," Marshall looked directly at his friend. "The guy's a snake and a poisonous one as well. The sooner you stomp on him, the safer for everyone. Even if the *Card* makes it, Winthrop will grab all the credit. He's been around the Navy long enough to know how to do it.

Believe me he's busily out there right now, hedging his bets both ways. Bob, I just hate to see you fall victim to a guy like that."

Captain Mills looked thoughtful for a moment then replied, "Thanks Mike, I appreciate the benefit of your thinking and it will not go unnoticed."

Captain Mills entered the front office of ComResDesDiv5 at 1245. The Admiral's female Yeoman greeted him warmly. "The Admiral asked that you go on in as soon as you got here." She arose and walked him to the Admiral's office door. She knocked then opened the door, took Captain Mills' hat and waited for the *Card's* skipper to step inside. She pulled the door closed and went back to her desk, placing Mills' hat on a hat rack that was standing by the outer door.

"Hello Bob," the seasoned Admiral said as he stood up and pushed his hand toward his visitor.

"Admiral," Captain Mills gripped the Admiral's hand and pumped it.

"I'm pressed for time so let's get down to business." The Admiral sat down. He pointed to a chair beside his desk. "I see you are living on board these days, good idea; you have to supervise this operation personally. As I told Buck when you took the job, those people need kicked in the butt, but we think there are some good people over there. Are you staying within your budget and your deadlines?"

"If my calculations are correct, we can be successful and within budget, but I am very concerned about the deadline, I may need more help than I have available on board."

"Do what you need to do Bob, just stay within budget, I have a boss too, you know. And I don't need to tell you where we will all be if you don't show up for the party in Gitmo."

"I am well aware of that Admiral."

"Bob, me and Buck's butts are in a sling because of Gallagher. Me, and the boys in the corner offices are really impressed with your management skills; you certainly took control of your company after your uncle and father died. We were impressed; too, with the help you gave us consulting on the *Richards*. Don't hesitate to call me if you need anything. I mean that. "Now . . . let's talk about John Winthrop. I know by now you have discovered what Buck meant when he said he was a problem for us . . . and the Winthrop family. But you know we think this boy will make a fine commander someday. He needs some maturity. He took quite a hit being assigned to the *Card*. As I said, Gallagher was not good for him, but we want you to square that young man away. I will be very interested in seeing your fitness reports on him as well as the others. You can surmise there are plans for that boy."

He leaned back in his chair and crossed his legs.

"Thornton and Dunhill (*Winthrop's Dad and Uncle*) are very interested in his professional growth and how this experience on the *Card* will play out. But we can't move him until he matures. That is your job, Bob.

Do the best you can but don't scuttle the *Card* in the process. If it comes down to it, and you have to relieve him, then, do what you must and Captain Sorenson and I will support you."

The Commander of the Reserve Destroyer Division 5 stood up.

The Captain of the *USS Card* stood up.

"You need anything from me?"

"No thank you Sir. I will let Captain Sorenson know if I run aground."

"I want you to. This little project is very important to the Division in general and squadron thirty-four in particular."
"I appreciate that Sir."

Captain Mills returned to the ship and called a special meeting of the ship's officers in the wardroom that afternoon.

He began the meeting congratulating the officer corps on their work. "Reports from the departments have shown remarkable progress, but getting repairs completed in time for getting underway during the next weekend looked slim indeed. We are an entire month behind schedule. We must do something drastic if we are going to meet our deadline."

Chapter 5 - Executive Assessment Battle Condition X-Ray

Contracting for Outside Services

The Card is in the *norming* stage of team development. Work is getting done, and the morale seems to be coming back. The fact that the ship needs to get skilled assistance from outside does not diminish the Norming operations. Can the U.S.S. Card accomplish the Captain's objectives with available personnel and materiel? With the help of Senior Chief Gruber, the answer was no. Too much time has been lost. The officers and crew were, now aware of their inability to complete the task without outside help.

Many managers are reluctant to contract for outside services believing that it shows a lack of planning and management ability. What determines when to call for outside consultants, technicians, contractors and other experts? Is it advisable to contract for outside services when there is talent available in house? The key decision factors are cost effectiveness and criticality of time and resources. If an outside contractor can do it faster with less expense, or at least with more cost effectiveness it may be advisable to use a contractor. If the project calls for resources that are not available on board, or special licenses not available in house. If the company is literally fighting for survival; the consultant can save critical weeks and even months in helping identify the best opportunities for rebuilding competitive position or imposing profitability. When the time factor is such that outside contractors can come in, do the job, clean up, take away the debris, and leave your operation functioning effectively the contract should be considered.

I will agree that cost should not be the only consideration. One must consider the affect this decision will have on those who would normally do this work. It could be interpreted as a vote of no-confidence so care must be taken when considering this action. Under conditions where the operation is running with competent personnel, and the need for an outside contractor is determined to be in the best interest of the organization, the manager in charge of the affected department should be the one who controls the hiring of the contractor and supervises the work. The situation in the engine room, calls for outside consultants, technicians, contractors and other experts to assist. Senior Chief Gruber welcomed the outside help.

Management Axiom:

In situations where disaster is the consequence for missing a required deadline, the executive must place one action before all others and insist on a successful outcome. In some cases this means putting the cost effectiveness aside and getting the work done at all costs. That one action in this case, is to get the Card underway at their next drill.

Chapter 6 - S.O.S
**Thursday, 09 April 1970
USS Card Pier Side
US Coast Guard Yard, Curtis Bay, Maryland**

The outside contractors swarmed around the ship, working with the ship's company and a group of selected reserves, the department head's plans and work orders were completed. Their work done, the contractors left the ship for the last time at Twenty One Hundred (9pm) Sunday 9, April.

By Wednesday, 12 April, all reports from the Engineering Department indicated that the ship would, in fact, be able to get underway that weekend. Lieutenant Commander McCormick busied himself, checking that all details and assignments had been finalized and reported the results to Captain Mills.

The main objective of the weekend cruise would be to test the ship's ability to operate on its own, but equally important in the mind of Captain Mills was to let the officers and crew members experience some successful results for their weeks of effort or for the officers and crew to experience failure that would clearly demonstrate their need to pay closer attention to those for which they are responsible.

Friday 14, April: When the ready reserves reported aboard for the April drill they were all wearing the ship's identification patch on the sleeve of the upper right shoulder. They were carrying AWOL bags with the Card's coat of Arms patch sewn on the side. The announced sea bag inspection revealed that all enlisted personnel had the ship's identification patch sewn on all their white and blue uniforms. The ship's coat of arms patch was sewn on all work jackets as ordered.

The ship's officers met in the wardroom to do the mandatory maneuvering walk-through in preparation for the next day's mission. Mr. Winthrop mapped out the ship's movement on the chart. The captain insisted that every range, every heading, every turn and degree of rudder, and the speed for each movement should be written out. Mr. Winthrop will take the ship out and be the first to qualify on the Card as a driver. After the Card was at sea, Mr. McCormick will take his turn at the controls for one hour, followed by Miss Grubaugh, then Miss Sterling, and down the chain until every officer on board had the necessary time in to qualify for maneuvering.

The maneuvering detail was ordered to the bridge where the movements out through the channel were rehearsed. The special sea and anchor detail went through a similar rehearsal. The engine room rehearsed the shift from shore power to ship power and the shifts of speeds that would be needed.

Saturday, 15, April, the *Card's* crew was making preparation for getting underway for the first time in over a year

At zero eight-hundred the boilers were producing the required steam pressure, all lines and fittings were holding, the generators kept a steady output and all required electrical and electronic systems had passed their functional checks and were operating on ship power. The engine room reported "ready for getting underway".

At Ten-hundred hours (10:00 AM) all was ready. Captain Mills was in his chair on the Port side of the bridge. The Executive Officer's chair, on the opposite side, was vacant as LCDR McCormick joined Lt. Grubaugh, Officer of the Deck, in observing the various workstations operating on the bridge. Lt. Winthrop stood by the console behind the windscreen; he was driving the ship or, as it's termed, he "had the conn".

The last mooring line was dropped and the Boatswain Mate of the Watch blew a long whistle blast and passed the word to shift colors. The Jack and ensign were hauled down smartly and the *steaming* ensign was hoisted on the gaff and the ship's call sign was hoisted.

There was a stirring of excitement among the many crewmen on deck as the lines were cast off. The only thing that kept them from total delight was the taunts and remarks from deck hands on the two Coast Guard tugs which were helping the *Card* out into the ship channel.

"If you want, we'll just stay with you. That way you won't have to call us when you need to get towed back in."

"Are you guys sure you can handle being out on the water?"

"It's been so long since you've been out; we thought you'd been transferred to the Army!"

"You won't like it out there. Carps aren't used to salt water."

As the Card glided into the middle of the ship channel, the tugs turned away and with one last round of wisecracks they steered back toward the Coast Guard yard. *Card* was underway, using her own power, her own steering, and her own crew.

It was an emotional moment for officers and the crew alike as they savored the rush of air and watched the tea-colored wake churning behind them.

Lt Winthrop looked every bit the professional naval officer as his eyes swept the ship channel and the various instruments on the bridge.

He issued engine and steering orders in a crisp and decisive manner, and had the *Card* in the proper position for taking the main ship channel around Hamilton Point.

It was approximately ten forty five, a half hour into the voyage the ship was surging headlong in the channel and then it began to slow dramatically. A voice from the intercom system broke in.

"Bridge, Engine room," said the voice.

"Bridge, go ahead," Winthrop replied.

"Sir, we've had a problem. We've lost boiler fire. We're attempting to re-light."

There was a stunned silence on the bridge. Of the ten people there, only Captain Mills looked at anyone else. He let another moment pass, and then toggled the switch on his intercom.

"Engine Room this is the Captain. What's your status?"

The red indicator had failed to light on the intercom box. Simultaneously the lights and all electrical instruments on the bridge went out. The Captain reached for the microphone on his voice-powered set and repeated the question.

A red light came illuminated on the consol in front Lieutenant Grubaugh. It was the power indicator of the emergency voice powered communication system between the engine room and the bridge.

"Captain, this is Chief Gruber. We've had a failure of the spring-loaded 'quick kill' fuel shut-off valve, Sir. The boilers went out and we're trying to start the diesel generator to get power back to the fuel pumps. We should be able to attempt re-light within two minutes."

The captain keyed his voice powered phone again. "Keep me appraised, Engine Room." The Captain sat back in his chair and looked straight ahead.

The *Card* was losing all forward momentum, and was beginning to drift sideways in the channel.

"Lieutenant Grubaugh," Captain Mills spoke over his shoulder, "notify the Coast Guard tug to stand by to render assistance."

"They're still in visual range," observed a Petty Officer from behind the navigation table, "we can contact them by hand-held radio or semaphore."

"Please do so from the bridge wing," said the Lieutenant without turning around. "You'll find the reception better from out there." She didn't want to hear the *Card's* call for help.

The darkness continued for several more minutes before the engine room reported again.

"This is Gruber. We didn't have enough stored start-air to get the diesel running, Sir. We're going to try one last trick."

"What's that?" asked the captain into the phone

"If the steam lines haven't cooled off too much, we can scavenge residual pressure into the generators and put out enough current to run the fuel pumps long enough to light-off the boilers."

"Keep me informed," the Captain spoke in a flat tone.

Another moment went by before the chief's voice returned. "I'm afraid we're going to stay as we are, Sir: Dead in the Water."

By now the ship had turned enough in the channel so the Captain could look out the side window by his chair and see the Coast Guard tug plowing through the water toward the *Card*.

McCormick had dispatched a Chief out on to the bridge wing where he was directing members of the crew in their preparations for sending a line over to the tug.

Even before the tug came along side they could hear the calls beginning. "Lookin' good, *Card*."

"Anyone get seasick yet?"

"You guys were that close to a new world's record!"

Phillips, a salty old Third Class Boatswain's Mate, had prepared the gun for shooting the line over to the tug. But instead of launching it into the empty area, he aimed at one of the most vocal of the tug's crew. The man ducked in time and the lead weight missed his head by inches.

"Get that man below!" Mr. McCormick ordered.

Boatswain mate Furman pulled Phillips inside. The remaining crewmembers worked in sullen silence, passing and securing the larger towing lines.

When the ship was brought into line behind the fleet tug and being towed back to the pier, Captain Mills turned around in his chair and addressing everyone on the bridge in general more than any one individual.

"After that last incident, I'll probably have some explaining to do to ComResDesRon. I should make an appearance to my friend the Commander of the Coast Guard Base. Until I return, everyone will be confined to the ship. No one leaves. No one comes aboard."

The Coast Guard Commander was glad Captain Mills came to see him. While the captain did not have to explain anything to the Coast Guard commander, he felt he owed it to him. He and the Coast Guard commander were not close friends, they were well acquainted and he felt he needed to maintain a good relationship with him, since he was Card's landlord (the Card was tied up at the CG pier).

"You have an unruly crew, Captain," the Rear Admiral began.

"I have a frustrated Crew Admiral." Mills replied. "As the Admiral knows, we've put a lot of time and effort into getting the *Card* back into operational status."

"The *Card* is not in operational status," the Admiral corrected.

"We're making head-way, Sir," the Captain persisted.

"You're kidding yourself, Commander. When a ship's been idle as long as the Card has been, it's only going to get operational again with a lot of outside help and a lot of money. Your ship's too old for the Navy to expend either on it. I'm surprised Buck Sorenson took it on. I hear you're a good turn-around man, but as good as you are Bob, I don't think you have had anything this far gone."

He pushed a white Coast Guard coffee mug toward the captain of the *Card*, and pointed to a silver coffee pot with a fancy "S" shaped spout. The coast guard insignia was etched into the pot. A very impressive piece.

Captain Mills held up his hand indicating "no thank you."

The Coast Guard boss leaned back in his chair. "Captain Gallagher was a realist. He knew the risks weren't worth it and he kept people just doing what training and qualification they could. People have been trying to tell you the same thing all along. Maybe now you can see what they've been saying."

Captain Mills was shaking his head. "Sir, ComResDesRon sent inspection crews aboard. They said it could be a fully functional ship with a reasonable amount of effort."

"Again, I think you're kidding yourself and your crew.

The squadron inspection team doesn't have to take the risks for failure. Your people do. And when they get their hopes built up over something that can't happen, that's when their frustration comes out like it did today.

That man of yours endangered the life of one of my crewmen. I hold you directly responsible for that."

"I'd never try to deny my responsibility for what happened out there today."

The Admiral's demeanor and voice softened noticeably.

"Bob," he said, "it's not necessary for anyone to be responsible for things like that. It's so unnecessary. You just have to be realistic about what the *Card* is. He leaned forward to emphasize his next point. It's a ship at the end of its useful life. The crew settled into mediocrity a long time ago. Your reserves are only there to play Navy and get retirement points, and every one of your Regulars is chomping at the bit to get reassigned."

"There isn't a thing any of the crew wants that they can't get from the *Card*," Captain Mills was still determined. "Her mission is to be combat-ready right up until she's decommissioned. Getting her there and keeping her that way can be the best thing we could do for everyone on board."

"So you're going to give 'em your 'Captain John Paul Jones I have not yet begun to fight' speech?" Huh?

Mills grinned and gave a shrug. "She was a fine old bucket in her day, and she needs go out in style, into a red sunset [*red sky at night a sailor's delight*] with her ensign flying, her crew standing in pride."

"Well, Bob, all I can say is 'fair winds'. And I hope you have better luck after that speech than John Paul Jones did after <u>he</u> gave it." The Admiral paused. "His ship sank the next morning."

"Admiral, I read a piece on you when I was a young Lieutenant. A reporter asked you what makes mariners go to sea and risk their lives on ships, and how is it the Coast Guard is willing to go out into a storm and rescue other ships at sea? I have never forgotten your answer. I have applied it in every aspect of my life. You said 'Son, a ship may be safe in the harbor, but that is not what ships are for.'"

"Well said Commander Mills well said. I guess you know what you're doing. I just didn't want to see your superlative record marred by this pirate ship.

The Admiral stood up.

Commander Mills stood up.

"Carry on, then Captain Mills . . . and fair winds."

"Thank you Admiral."

ComResDesRon did not acknowledge the event so captain Mills chose not to visit his office.

While Captain Mills was off the ship, things on board the Card were in turmoil. Tempers flared and vocabularies subsided into a few well-worn profanities.

The Chiefs kept up a walking patrol throughout the ship after several incidents of destructive violence, including a mass throwing of dishes in the enlisted dining area.

The situation in the wardroom was not much better. Lieutenant Winthrop was holding court on the events of the day.

"I wish he'd listened to us from the beginning, we wouldn't have had this humiliation in front of the whole world."

"Boy, if morale was bad before! It's going to be terrible now," Lieutenant Fridel added loyally.

Grubaugh wasn't in the mood for it. "Morale was bad before Mills got here because we were a bunch of losers. We sat out the Squadron exercises. We had no chance for promotion..."

"And it's better now?" Winthrop broke in. "Just listen to how things are on this ship right now! If you haven't seen the light yet, just go take a look in the mess deck. That'll wake you up!"

Lt. Grubaugh was shaking her head. "Those feelings didn't develop overnight. No one's felt good about this ship for a long time. No, the man has a point. This is at least a chance to do something instead of just sitting on our butts and grumbling about fate."

Winthrop was leaning back, feeling confident now. "You're being naive and over-idealistic, Phil *(sometimes the officers shortened her name to Phil, but there was no disrespect intended)*. I know what it takes to get promoted, and I also know that no matter what else you may want to believe, that's got to come before everything else. Not only will your actions fail to get to the top, but your ideas will never get there either."

The usually quiet acquiescent Marshall Goldsmith surprised them all when he spoke up;

"No but the captain's ideas will. He has been a big help to me and my department, and if you think about it he has been good for all of us."

Lt. Sterling had listened to this exchange in the same silence as the other officers in the wardroom, but now she stood up.

"You know," she began, folding her arms, "this reminds me so much of what happened back on our soccer team in college.

You didn't know I played soccer did you? We would wrangle among ourselves like this for two seasons and spent both those seasons at the bottom of our conference."

"The alumni finally got enough of it and we had a new coach; a guy who came in, like Mills, only stronger. He really kicked our butts, didn't let us alone for a minute. He'd say, 'you've been a bunch of losers because that's what you've felt like, told yourselves you were, and acted like. When you're doing that, you're going to be losers.'"

All eyes were following Sterling now as she walked to the head of the wardroom table and continued.

"But what that coach did was to make us look beyond ourselves to what was the purpose." She paused and looked at Winthrop.

"We didn't want to do it at first, and we bucked him as best we could, but in the end we came around to his way of thinking."

Now Sterling shook her head, looked up at the overhead and spread her arms, smiling broadly as she did so.

"You guys can't imagine what a thrill it is to stand out there on the field at the Pan Am Games facing the Cubans, the best team in the International League. We didn't think we were good enough for the Atlantic Coast Conference, and now here we were playing the best of the International League. We had come this far, winning every game and qualifying to represent the U.S. at the Pan Am games. We didn't beat the Cubans, but it took 3 overtimes before they beat us. And that would not have happened then, if our first string goalie had not gotten injured."

She looked back down at the officers seated around the table. "I never felt that good before or since. But that's what Mills is trying to do for us.

He's going to turn this ship and crew around and the only thing you can do by bucking him is make a fool of yourself."

Her expression changed, as though she just thought of something that had never occurred to her before this.

She placed the knuckles of both hands on the wardroom table and leaned in toward the others.

"You say the plan the captain is using will not work? Think about it. That plan has gotten us under way in spite of the resistance. That is something we haven't done in two years. What he needs now is the extra effort by the crew to do their jobs. He has exposed the problems as being inattention **not** incompetence. We can do it; we just need to want to. All the frustration that is being exhibited today is evidence that the enlisted know it. They just need a chance. And that chance must come from us."

Mister Cavatini offered his endorsement; "Well said Lieutenant Sterling, Hear Here".

Mister Cavatini's expression turned to one of deep thoughtfulness.

"I wonder how much of that ruckus in the enlisted ranks was because of the ship's sad state of affairs, and how much of it was a protest of the ship's management team?"

Sterling rapped her knuckles on the table surface with an air of finality, then turned and left the wardroom. Grubaugh followed a moment later without a word.

The Captain returned to the ship and the normal ship-board routine commenced.

At sixteen hundred (4:00 PM) the days working hours were secured and the normal watch standing routine commenced and the crew was on-their own but all liberty was cancelled. (They were not allowed to leave the ship)

On Sunday 16 April the day's work began at ten hundred (10:00 AM). The captain instructed Mister McCormick to order each department head to conduct sea-going emergency drills, dead-in-water drills. The ships training exercises ceased at twelve thirty for chow. At Fourteen hundred (2:00 PM) Department heads met with their crews to go over the results of drills and set the agenda for next month's drill weekend. At sixteen thirty (4:30) the drill weekend was secured and all ready reserve hands were dismissed from duty. They left the ship along with the regular Navy crew who were granted liberty for the evening.

The captain left the ship at seventeen hundred (5:00 PM). The other reserve officers and the officers of the regular ship's company were sitting around the wardroom table engaged in squaring away their drill reports, drinking coffee and preparing for the next drill weekend.

Mister Goldsmith looked up from his files and said: "We have made a lot of progress, but we still haven't been able to complete any assignment. The Captain needs us to step up. What do you think?"

There was silence in the wardroom. The two lady officers just looked at each other but did not offer an opinion. They had made their thoughts known and now the ball was in the men's courts.

Mr. Hooper broke the silence. Without looking up from his papers he said; "I was as certain as the rest of you that the captain's plan was doomed to failure, not because the plan was bad, but I didn't think his management style was effective. What has all this resistance gotten us?

Tethered to the back of a Coast Guard Cutter with no canvas up, like a bunch of Sea Scout recruits. *No canvas up- old mariner's jargon for no wind for propulsion)* Grubaugh and Sterling are right. It's time we got with the captain's program".

He clicked the point of his ball point pen in place, signed his name to the report, and clicked the point back into the pen.

He placed it in his pocket, folded the paper, and without looking at any one, he stood up, placed the report in his report slot at the project control area, and left the room.

Mister Fridel turned to face Mr. Winthrop. "John, I still believe most of the officers and men are not completely on board with the Captain's plan, and maybe it **is** because of his passive management style. In any case maybe we can help the captain, by offering alternative suggestions to his plan. If we met in an open session, where we could speak freely, you know, brainstorm, maybe we could come up with some ideas the captain can agree to, and take off some of the pressure. He is under the gun from ComResDesRon and that puts us all under the gun to do something ComResDesRon does not realize cannot be done."

"That may be an idea whose time has come." Mr. Winthrop added.

"The announcement about the meeting will need to come from you, as the OIC, Fridel added. I will pass the word among the officers and you invite the captain. Let him know what we want to do and we are cooperating."

On Monday, Robert Mills returned to his corporate office to take care of problems and routine business that had come up during his absence.

He met with his management staff and made sure operations would continued for the next few weeks while he devoted his time to preparing the ship for the shakedown cruise. On Tuesday, he spent the morning and the lunch period in meetings with the Executive Vice President of his company.

Robert Mills returned to his executive office, after lunch on Tuesday afternoon, he settled in determined to take a respite from the constant stress of the "Card Project", and handle a few Benchmark group items that only he could authorize. He knew the bulk of administrative actions were dispatched flawlessly by Marge Brubaker his competent administrative assistant. She had been handling this part of the business for the past 20 years. His uncle and father often said she was not just the administrative assistant and office manager she was the business manager.

He sat in the big cordovan colored leather executive chair and surveyed the office he inherited. The office was old world elegance with dark cherry colored leather upholstered chairs and sofa. There was even a fireplace his grandfather had installed when he refurbished the room almost twenty years ago. On the mantel was a model of a seventeenth century tall ship with a three foot mast. There was a faint smell of leather and of his father's pipe tobacco that still lingered. Mills "took in" the plush carpets, polished oak walls and walnut casework. The room lent itself to the hush of power that had been passed down through three generations of Mills to this successor, who in turn is expected to hand it down to the next worthy successor.

He noticed an envelope on his desk bearing the *U.S.S. Card*'s seal. He removed the contents. It was a note written on official ship's stationery.

"The ship's company officers are meeting for dinner tonight with the reserve officers in the *Sea Fearer* room at *The Wharf*. We will be discussing our situation and methods for dealing with it. Your presence is respectfully requested."

 John D. Winthrop, Lt. USN
Officer in Charge
U.S.S. Card DE 383

Chapter 6 Executive Assessment S.O.S

Disappointment, Criticism and Defeat

It would appear that the Captain has suffered a major defeat. He was counting on taking the ship and crew out to sea to let them experience a success, but they only experienced more failure - and a public one at that. The crew had to be embarrassed for themselves. Surely they knew neither they nor the ship was seaworthy and they had only themselves to blame. They will blame the Captain. He was the one that provided the opportunity for the humiliation. They will also blame Lieutenant Winthrop and Commander McCormick because they will realize it was these managers that allowed the deterioration of the ship and the crew's competence.

But the Captain had to try it. If the operation would have been successful that would have been well and good, but if the outcome was to be unsuccessful it would serve to show the officers and crew where their problems were and what had to be done to correct it.

Had they not tried it, they would still be unaware of their incapability for handling a ship at sea. Better have the problem now, than to find it the day before they were to sail for the exercise.

Those officers and crew who were still resisting the captain's efforts will take this event with glee. The senior manager must be (or appear to be) calm with personal emotions in check and issue orders that will get the situation under control. Every person involved in the disappointment must be accountable for their part in the failure. The executive's credibility will be greatly influenced by one's deportment in the face of the defeat, or mishap. There is an old adage that goes "Don't let them see you sweat." It is ok to show disappointment in the outcome of some project, but never show disappointment in yourself or those who were carrying out your orders. The last thing the executive in charge has time for is self-pity, no matter how tumultuous the current experience. Those thoughts must be suppressed. The officers and crew must never know about those thoughts.

In addition to public humiliation, the captain is under a lot of criticism by everyone involved. How does a senior manager handle criticism? Criticism will come, but the real problem with criticism is discouragement. The manager must avoid the tendency to compare themselves with what the others are saying. Critics throw obstacles in our path that perplex us and confuse us. They try to keep us off balance. Obstacles are those frightening things we see when we take our eyes off our goal. Sometimes critics come disguised as confidants who use critical sophistry to convince others that the true leader is unfit to lead. It is easy to find fault. When it appears that a manager has fallen from grace, vultures descend on the situation to jockey for a protective position.

They want to focus on the manager under fire, in order to keep others from focusing on their own short comings. Leaders encourage, critics demoralize. How do we handle criticism?

"Anyone who steps into the arena of leadership must be prepared to pay a price. True leadership exacts a heavy toll on the whole person - and the more effective the leadership, the higher the price. The leader must soon face the fact that he will be the target of critical darts. Unpleasant though it may sound, you haven't really led until you have become familiar with the stinging barks of the critic. Good leaders must have thick skin." Charles Swindoll, <u>Hand Me Another Brick</u> page 69.

More often than not the critic did not have a clear perception of the situation or the senior manager's position or limitations. And while the critic can attack the current plan it is rare that the critic has any real plans for dealing with the situation.

Should the Captain persist in his approach, or should he change tactics? Effective managers are perceived by others as uncompromising, unswerving in the pursuit of mission attainment. The captain must hang in there. That is what he was hired to do. The executive's job is not an easy one. The effective executive must take a disciplined stand for stick-to-itiveness. Persistence wears down opposition and in the absence of opposition, one wins.

The ship captain, like any chief executive may be the loneliest job on earth. The chief executive is greatly outnumbered, with only the power of the position and his own resolve for support. When all is said and done there is no substitute for personal will. Once the will is lost . . . all is lost.

That perception cannot be based on mere image. It must reflect a genuine deep personal commitment to duty. Every manager must realize that opposition will come - - it is inevitable. George Patton once said; *"The only test that counts for an officer is how he behaves when people are shooting at him."*

Several years ago Hollywood released the movie *Memphis Belle*, the final bombing mission of a B-17 crew during World War II. The aircraft sent as the replacement for the Belle was flying their first mission with the Belle. When they crossed into enemy territory they came under heavy *flack* from anti-aircraft artillery. The shells were exploding at their altitude creating great turbulence and damage to the bombers. The radio operator of the replacement plane called the radio operator on the Belle and said "They have our altitude and our air speed we are sitting ducks up here, why doesn't the pilot get us out of this flack? Why doesn't he go higher, out of range, or fly faster so they can't track our airspeed?"

The answer the Belle's radio operator gave him is priceless. To paraphrase his answer he said; "Our mission is to drop bombs on specific targets. To do that the bombardier must accurately calculate the trajectory and co ordinance. That means the pilot must hold the plane steady at a certain speed and altitude in spite of the flack. As frightening and dangerous as it is to achieve the mission bomber pilots must learn to fly through the flack." That is an excellent metaphor for managing in turbulent times. To achieve a successful outcome for the mission the executive in charge must learn to fly through the flack.

Taking the initiative to lead out, to assume responsibility, will bring rewards if successful, but it is fraught with peril, because the manager carries the burden of management, leadership and the responsibility for success and failure. Failure in itself isn't terrible. Not learning from failure is the terrible part of failure. Repeating the same mistakes is catastrophic. Moving forward smartly, adjusting as necessary is the mark of the effective manager and the true leader. In situations such as this, and with little cooperation one would almost wonder if the organization and its managers are worth the effort.

How could this happen? Before a senior manager approves the go-ahead on a major high profile project there should be ample evidence that success is highly probable. They are aware of the potential problems and have back up plans to handle all contingencies. In this case Captain Mills anticipated the problem and due to his continuous inspections of the engine room and meetings with Senior Chief Gruber, he prepared for just such a contingency.

He was aware that the ship could lose power in the bay. The officers and the crew needed to see for themselves that they could be successful with a little more training and more work on their particular jobs on the ship.

He thought the humiliation would motivate them into action an action directed toward applying themselves to getting their area of the ship sea worthy.

They could see themselves making progress. Their fervor for competence training had given them new level of confidence. They could feel the exhilaration of possible success.

They, once again, were willing to identify with their ship, to wear its name on their uniforms and the coat of arms on their work jackets and civilian clothing. They were ready, willing and becoming able to make a substantial contribution toward making the Card a dependable, sea-going American defensive weapon again. They were looking forward to fulfilling their mission to "Seek – Strike and Prevail".

Prior to this test the crew had operated and failed in anonymity with no consequences. This failure occurred out in the open where it could be observed opening them up to public scrutiny and the consequences of their failure. A great disappointment such as this could have been the final blow to the crew's morale, or it could have just been the thing to spark a new level of commitment. The Captain took the risk. He knew they would not make it to the open sea.

If you did your homework, and you made the best decision you could based on the information available to you at the time, then you have done all anyone can do. Of course it is axiomatic that the senior manager will have a backup plan when the task has a significant chance of failure. The plan does not have to be tested but the "course" should be known. In this case the captain had the coast guard tugs out of sight but available. Far enough away to give his crew the feeling of aloneness and vulnerability but close enough to rescue them before they would get into a life threatening situation.

The next step is to analyze the situation. What happened that was different from what we expected?

Now how do we get the outcomes we want? Formulate a new plan. Call in your trusted subordinates or peers to give you "the benefit of their thinking". We do not need advice at this point, we only need different perspectives. Department heads should determine what they did to contribute to the problem and issue assignments to their crew that will get their minds off the defeat and onto correction.

The captain allowed the crew to see that he meant business and they could come up to the standard. He could not have done it sooner. He needed to bring them up to this state of readiness. He employed pertinacity, the tenacity to keep pertinent issues in motion, combined with the determination to see the mission through at all costs, with doggedness and patience.

The organization is the goose that lays the golden eggs; the primary objective of each member is to take care of the goose. The managers and the crew must come up to the standards necessary for success and it is the responsibility of the senior manager to make that happen. The final outcome must be a successful achievement and it is worth the effort!

There is yet another situation that needs attention. There appears to be a clique in the officer ranks. Winthrop, McCormick, Fridel, Hooper and Winchester appear to have their own agenda and have formed a confederacy in order to promote that agenda. Cavatini, Sterling and Grubaugh appear to have formed a confederacy to protect themselves against the others. Mr. Goldsmith does not seem to either have the time or interest in allying with either of them.

People form cliques when they feel a need for security, protection against a situation they feel is threatening to their comfort level. Nothing is more damaging, more forbidden in the management team than a clique. They undermine the legitimate authority.

Then there was the meeting! Standing tall and being the stanchion has not been easy, getting their cooperation met with resistance, assembling the project team and getting them to buy in was like pulling teeth, now the captain is faced with what appears to be a conspiracy. The officers, led by the Officer-In-Charge, Lieutenant Winthrop, at the suggestion of Lieutenant Fridel, decided to hold a meeting and the Captain's invitation sounded more like an order that a request. Even though he is the officer in charge he does not hold that designation with the captain. Signing it "Officer-in-Charge" reeks of command usurpation, a very dangerous action to be sure. How should the captain respond to this?

As enticing as it may appear, the captain should not attend the meeting. His presence would lend legitimacy to the proceedings. The captain has veto power, and no decisions that could affect the management of the organization, made by subordinate managers can be carried out without the chief executive's approval.

His absence will speak volumes and should strike fear in the hearts of those who do attend, as they will realize that if they can't manipulate the senior manager to acquiesce.

This action, on the part of the subordinate managers is tantamount to mutiny at worst and insubordination at best.

His blatant absence will send the message that the captain is not interested in deviating from the plan and by ignoring the situation he provides an opportunity for them to escape the consequences in spite of their lack of prudent judgment. He could have put them all on report, but he chose to remain silent. They now realized how vulnerable they really are.

How should the captain respond to his discovery of Winthrop's "flanking maneuver" through headquarters? The manager can never stay balanced fighting a comparison battle. Lieutenant Winthrop's flanking maneuver has not gone without notice, from the captain, the crew, the officers, ComResDesRon and top management at the Navy base. The captain has a plan, it is working. Top management believes in his plan.

The crew now realizes his plan can work and they can be successful if they cooperate with him. Mr. Winthrop is taking rope with which to swing into success, but if he persists on his current course it will be the rope that will hang him. There comes a time, with every rebellious or maverick subordinate manager when they realize that they were only fooling themselves, and jeopardizing their careers. Mr. Winthrop will soon realize, if he hasn't already, that he had gone too far and the one person who can destroy him is the only one who can save him.

Rule of Command #9
Never show fear in the face of difficult situations, never show defeat in the face of failure.

Rule of Command # 10
Maintain *pertinacity*. In situations where disaster is the consequence for continuing current practices, the executive must place one action before all others and insist on a successful outcome. This will require will power. Without will power the effort cannot be sustained.

Management Axiom:
The effective executive must take a disciplined stand for stick-to-itiveness. Persistence wears down opposition, and in the absence of opposition, one wins. Pertinacity must be continuously employed. This is the tenacity to keep pertinent issues in motion, combined with the determination to see the mission through at all costs, with doggedness and patience. To achieve a successful outcome for the mission the executive in charge must learn to fly through the flack.

Learn from your mistakes. Individual failures won't defeat you. Repeated *failures* will. A mistake or mishap becomes a defeat when we start blaming others. Have faith in your own judgment, even if it appears that your judgment was lacking in this situation. You will always be right more often than you are wrong, and even when you are wrong the situation is rarely beyond repair.

The surprise meeting invitation from Lieutenant Winthrop brings up another absolute rule of command:

Rule of Command #11
Never, never, never surprise the boss!

Chapter 7 Flank Speed

Tuesday, 14 April, 1970
Wardroom - USS Card, Pier Side
US Coast Guard Yard, Curtis Bay Maryland

1200: Lieutenant Winthrop was anxious to get a reading from the other officers regarding the attendance at the last night's meeting at the Warf Restaurant. He placed a call to all the reserve officers and personally invited the officers of the ship's company.

They sat for lunch around the wardroom table. Mister Winthrop occupied the Captain's chair since he was the chair of the meeting. Next to him and to the left Lieutenant Commander McCormick occupied his usual seat. He was in a dress suit and tie. His plans were to dispense with this meeting as quickly as possible and get back to his office. He had one very important item he needed to attend to. Lieutenant Grubaugh sat across from him. Across from her Lieutenant Sterling sat. She was in civvies as she was taking a long lunch break to be at the meeting. Next to Lieutenant Grubaugh sat Lieutenant Fridel. Lieutenant (jg) Goldsmith sat next to him and across from Lieutenant (jg) Hooper. Lieutenant (jg) Winchester sat across from Hooper, and Ensign Cavatini sat next to him. He wanted to get this meeting over and done with before the captain reported aboard. He was expected at 1400 this afternoon. His agenda was to discuss the results of last night's meeting and get consensuses on what to do next.

"Well last night's meeting was a dismal failure," Mister Winthrop began.

"What happened?" asked Lieutenant Sterling. She chose not to attend. Claimed she had an important event at work and could not miss it.

"I can say I am very disappointed that you and Lieutenant Grubaugh chose to ignore the invitation to explore strategies that would assist the Captain in getting this ship in order. I want you to know your abandonment will not go unnoticed. I can understand Lieutenant Sterling's absence, she had pressing business at the office, but Phil you have no excuse."

Lieutenants Grubaugh and Sterling said nothing.

"Mister Cavatini and Mister Hooper and Commander McCormick were there and they have important jobs outside the *Card.*"

"The meeting was bust," said Lieutenant Fridel. "The Captain didn't show up. He has always been willing to listen to us before."

"For him to show up would have given the meeting legitimacy. Perhaps the Captain did not get the invitation or maybe he didn't think a concerted effort by subordinate officers was a legitimate activity," added Sterling.

Mister Fridel continued uninterested in Sterling's perceptions on the matter. "I expected him to show up in full dress uniform and read us the riot act, or show up in civvies and take our suggestions seriously.

Even if he didn't agree with us at least he could have given us a good hearing."

"He could have done that, Mister Fridel," said Commander McCormick, in a low monotone voice. "Or he could have come in and had us all arrested for mutiny."

The officers' expressions clearly showed disbelief and shock. A cloud of real fear spread like wildfire around the wardroom table.

"That did not occur to me until I got home, and read the ship board Command and Control Operations Manual," McCormick continued. "It appears to me the Captain did us all a big favor by not showing up. What I am most concerned about now is what he will do about the meeting, and those of us who attended, when he comes on board this afternoon. I was a fool to forget this is a military vessel under military law and US Navy tradition. I want you all to know that if the Captain doesn't hang me, from this minute on he will be my Mohammad and I will be his prophet. Now you all will excuse me, I have to get to my office." He stood up and without hesitation exited the wardroom door, descended the ladder to the main deck off the ship and into his car.

Tuesday, 14 April 1970
McCormick and Stanberry Real Estate office
Glen Burnie, Maryland

1430: Mike McCormick was sitting at his desk at the real estate firm working on a problem for one of his clients. His thoughts were interrupted by the sound of an electronic click and the spontaneous illumination of the intercom light.

"Mr. McCormick, Marge Brubaker on line one returning your call."

"Thank You Cindy." He pulled the receiver next to his ear and spoke. "Miss Brubaker, this is Mike McCormick the Executive Officer on the *USS Card*. Robert Mills has asked me to evaluate the organizational assessments from our department heads. Would your office have any instructions or guidelines for assessment evaluators?" There was a pause. "You do? Outstanding! How can I get a copy? "You will? That would be great. Do you have my address? Oh you do? Yes I have a fax machine. Oh you can? Terrific! My number is . . . oh. Okay. Yes thank you, I appreciate that very much. Oh no, don't bother him, I will see him in a few days at our week end drill. Thanks again Miss Brubaker. Good Day."

Tuesday, 14 April 1970
Wardroom - USS Card, Pier Side
US Coast Guard Yard, Curtis Bay Maryland

1800: Captain Mills reported aboard and went straight to his cabin. He told his steward he would be taking dinner there. He had no contact with any of the officers or crew until 2000 when he ordered the galley to send coffee and ge-dunk to radio central. He listened for the steward to deliver the goods. "Compliments of the Captain," he said. Radioman Anderson took the goods. "Tell him thanks."

He let the door close as the steward turned to leave. The Captain entered the entrance code on the security pad outside and pushed the door open. Radioman Anderson, Yeoman Williams and Radarman Henson snapped to attention when they realized their visitor was the Captain.

"What's the occasion Captain?" Anderson asked.

"I like to snack when I read the news, and I don't like snacking alone. And, no offense, but my coffee is far superior to yours."

"Well, sir, you came to the right guys. We will help you eat these ge-dunks," Williams responded.

Anderson printed out Armed Forces News and the captain read as the sailors completed their publication updates.

Friday, 24 April 1970
USS Card Pier Side
US Coast Guard Yard, Curtis Bay, Maryland

The Captain was in the wardroom next to the *War-Room* project control area. There was a knock on the door, it opened and Engineman Senior Chief Gruber entered. His hat was tucked up under his left arm and a stack of papers in his right hand. "Good morning Captain."

"Good Morning Senior Chief, what have you there?"

"I brought the EDL's from the engine room to give to Mr. McCormick sir. I am sorry we are late getting them in, but we ran out of EDL forms and had to order more."

"I understand your situation Senior Chief. You may leave them with me."

"Very well sir." He placed the forms in the engineering basket and turned to face the Captain. "By your leave Captain."

"Thank You Senior Chief, is that all you have for us?"

"Yes Captain."

"Then thank you again chief, that will be all."

The Chief turned and walked out the door, pulling it closed behind him.

Captain Mills called a meeting with the officers in the wardroom. He ordered them to appear in their white uniforms rather than the khaki work uniform. They assembled in their summer dress white uniforms, starched with the prominent military creases in their proper place.

Anxiety hovered over the wardroom like a wet blanket. Officer eyes searched around the room without moving their heads. They suspected the order to appear in dress whites had something to do with the meeting the Captain chose not to attend. They were right.

"We are approaching the deadline for filing our report of intention concerning our participation in the exercise off Guantanamo. That report is due two months before the squadron is to rendezvous at Jacksonville." Captain Mills had been scanning the faces of his officers seated around the table as he spoke. He could see the fear in their faces and he could sense their shallow breathing. That was exactly what he wanted to see. He now looked down at the notepad in front of him and tapped the eraser of his pencil thoughtfully.

"That report will show our intentions; whether we mean to join the combat readiness exercise or if we'll sit it out dockside for another year." He looked back up at the officers. "The decision to go carries with it the promise that the *Card* can keep up with the squadron and that it can make the trip all the way there, and all the way back, and more importantly, that it can make a substantial contribution to the exercise scenario. The decision to stay tied up here is admitting failure. Failure to do the job we were hired to do."

Mills stopped and looked around the table for a reaction. Goldsmith and Hooper shifted uncomfortably in their chairs; Grubaugh, Cavatini and Sterling were all nodding and returning the Captain's gaze. The others remained quiet until Lieutenant Winthrop took the advantage.

"I for one, recommend we stand down, cut our losses, and give ComResDesRon a realistic appraisal of our situation and ask that we spend this year getting the ship and the crew ready for next year. This will give us plenty of time to prepare for a successful GITMO exercise next year."

Sterling's voice cut in like a klaxon, "I say we go for it!"

All heads turned to look at the Lieutenant, who then continued. "Whether we stay here, try it and fail, or whether we leave the *Card* for mothballs and get ourselves assigned to another ship, we're still losers and that's a fact. Let's be honest about it. The only way we can possibly win is to pull this ship together, make it to GITMO and back."

Winthrop didn't answer, but was less-than subtle as he flopped back in his chair, let out an inaudible sigh and rolled his eyes heavenward. It was Cavatini who did answer. "In bocca al lupo." His hand gesture was pure Italian. "Fortune lies in the mouth of the wolf." The rest of the officers sat silently. This was a new arrangement of alliances.

It was Lieutenant Commander McCormick who spoke next. "U.S. Grant was the General in Chief of the Army during the siege of Richmond. He issued many orders to his subordinate generals to take actions that would constantly press the Confederates. Almost all of them ended with the phrase *'much is now expected'*. I think now is the time for us to adopt that as our byword. If there ever was a time in our tenure on the *Card* when much is expected from all of us, it is now."

No one commented, but facial expressions showed relief and agreement.

The captain spoke next. "We can't approach this as risk taking.

We must approach it in as deliberate and systematic a way as we can. I want to get underway on the drill weekend of 8 May. We will sail south to Patuxent River Naval Base. We will give the crew liberty and Navy Exchange privileges.

We will then have a three-day shakedown cruise beginning from 22 to 24 May. We will then proceed to the firing range at Little Creek where we will spend one day doing mock gunnery exercises in preparation for the real gunnery exercise the next day, 26 May. I know it is not a drill weekend. It will be a special call-up. We will schedule a dependent's cruise on the Sunday of the drill week end on 14 June, and we'll sail for Jacksonville to join the squadron on 9 July."

McCormick's facial expression showed concern; "Captain that means calling in over half of our reserve enlisted and all of our reserve officers for the shakedown cruise."

"That's correct," Mills replied. "See to it Mister Goldsmith if you please." Then without noticeable break he continued. "Mister Winthrop, have you reviewed our schedules for squadron activities with ComResDesRon34?"

Winthrop shook his head, "Not yet, Captain."

Captain Mills gave a short nod. "Draft an operation schedule for the cruise on 8 May. I'll review it as soon as you're done. I'd like to have it on ComResDesRon's desk by close of business next Tuesday."

Lieutenant Fridel shifted in his chair. "Captain," he began, shaking his head as he spoke. "I don't know if you felt it, but I certainly did. When we had to get towed back in by the tug, it took the heart right out of everyone on this ship. It took the wind right out of my sails. You talk about killing morale that just about did us in."

"That lesson should have been enough for all of us!" Mister Winthrop chimed in. "This ship is just too steeped in bad luck."

Captain Mills placed his forearms on the table and looked directly at Mister Fridel as he spoke. "If you'd like to talk about the lessons of that weekend Mister Fridel, this might be the best time to do it." He stood up. "In the first place, I learned that we still need to look more aggressively and thoroughly at all areas of this ship. Your boilers, Mister Fridel went out because the 'quick-kill' fuel shut-off valve closed of its own accord. The quality control inspectors from the Navy Yard inspected the mechanism. The spring-tension was way out of adjustment."

Lieutenant Fridel shifted in his chair.

"Our technicians may or may not have used a torque wrench when setting it. There's no way to tell. But even so, that might not have made a difference. Every single one of our torque wrenches was out of calibration."

The Captain was jabbing the tabletop with his finger for emphasis.

"Of course, that mistake by itself wouldn't have caused all the trouble. Next, the diesel failed to start for the back-up generator. The gauge showed it had the proper load of 150 P.S.I. in the start-air tank." He paused and gave an artificial smile. "In fact it kept on showing 150 P.S.I. even after we opened the stopcock and drained the last of the air out of it."

The captain stood up and walked toward the counter. The new position put him directly behind Mister Fridel's chair. Mister Fridel shifted his position in order to better view the captain. The others who were disadvantaged by his new position made the necessary adjustments. The Captain turned toward his staff. He deliberately met the eyes of each one around the table.

"I wonder how many of our other gauges and valves are jammed like that? Something to think about, isn't it?"

He swung around toward Mister Fridel again; his face was no more than a yard's distance the from Lieutenant's face.

"But of course, that wasn't the end of it. There was still a procedure for scavenging off enough residual steam pressure into the regular generators to run the fuel pumps long enough to re-light the boilers. But we didn't do it."

He pointed a finger upward. "Training problem! Only the chiefs had ever heard of the procedure, and none of them had practiced it in years. Training and coordination," he repeated. The finger was now down and pointing at Mister Winthrop. "You call this bad luck Mister Winthrop. You may be right, but the fact remains that people make their own luck. And if ours is bad it's because we've made it that way."

His facial expression betrayed his anger. No one had ever seen this side of him and it caused great consternation. He was silent for what seemed like a long time. He regained his composure and in a more genteel tone he said; "Gentlemen.... he turned toward Sterling and Grubaugh . . . and Ladies. Now we've got work to do, and it's not going to get done by people who spend their time wallowing around in self-pity. We need to channel the same amount of creative energy into getting the *Card* seaworthy as we've spent in thinking up reasons why we can't. He paused again. His expression took on an air of finality. "And those who can't will be replaced."

The captain sat down in his chair and turned to face Winthrop again. There was a pause. In a low tone he asked: "Were there any further lessons of that experience you want to bring up, Lieutenant?"

"Winthrop shook his head. "No, Sir." His voice was barely audible.

Lieutenant Commander McCormick moved forward in his chair and cleared his throat. All eyes went to him. "The Captain is forging a weapon here. And we have forgotten a very important fact. We chose the Navy as our career, and that career has put us in the management of a US Naval Warship.

We are obliged to live by its demands. So without further discussion we will hear what the captain has in mind for us."

The Captain turned his attention to McCormick. "Thanks Mack."

"Mack?" McCormick thought to himself. "Hmm."

The captain continued. "We will take some of the contract technicians, who are now working on the propulsion system with us as we set sail during the drill weekend on the 8th to the 10th. I want to test out as many of our systems as we can under exercise conditions."

He turned to face Lieutenant Winthrop. "Mister Winthrop, I want you to detail and schedule at least three major exercises. Include each of the weapons systems on board. The first ones may be single-event exercises. If you think they'll provide the best experience, but I want the last ones to be multiple-system, integrated events. Lt Sterling will work closely with Lt Grubaugh to match the firing exercises up with appropriate command-and-control scenarios and messages through the CIC."

He scanned the faces of Lieutenants Grubaugh and Sterling. Then back to his Damage Control Officer. "Mister Winchester, each of the firing exercises should be followed up by a damage control exercise. Again, I want as complete a spectrum of events as is practical. Each of the departments on this ship should also have at least one major drill planned and scheduled for that time-period as well. Mr. Winthrop will provide over-all coordination for the integration and sequencing of these exercises."

Commander McCormick shuffled papers, his puzzled look gave notice he was obviously looking for something.

"You have something else Mack?" the captain asked.

"Yes Captain . . . ah . . . just a minute. Oh, yes, here." He selected one of the papers and perused it. "I almost missed this one. According to the ComResDesDiv instructions we are to have an Unrep exercise before we go."

"I thought I remembered reading that. Can we schedule it during the shakedown period?" the Captain asked.

"I will see what I can do Captain."

We will meet here again at 1500 hours next Friday. I will ask each of you to brief the rest of the staff on your exercise scenarios. Lieutenant Commander McCormick, you will run that meeting."

He paused, and then concluded, "I'm certain you will have a number of questions between now and next weekend.

Our Executive Officer will be available to provide you with all of the guidance you need. In the meantime, we all need to get back to work."

Captain Mills pushed back his chair and stood up. Immediately all other officers in the room followed suit and stood at attention while the Captain turned, retrieved his cap from the hat shelf and placed it under his left arm.

"Mister Winthrop you will join me on the bridge in five minutes." He turned and left the wardroom.

When Lieutenant Winthrop arrived on the bridge the captain was sitting in the Captain's chair on the port side of the bridge. He swiveled around to face the errant OIC. The Captain remained seated as Mister Winthrop stood at attention.

"Mister Winthrop this is where the action takes place when the ship is underway. If you ever want to be a part of that action again, you will discontinue your resistance to my command and my plans for this ship and its crew."

Captain Mills leaned back in his chair, folded his arms over his chest. His facial expression gave the distinct impression that he was deadly serious.

"You will subordinate yourself as a junior officer to his Commanding Officer. Is that understood?"

Mister Winthrop stood silent and seemed stunned by what he had just heard. "Captain Mills, all my life I have been groomed for a naval command. I have not been insubordinate; I have provided the benefit of my thinking for your consideration, and . . ."

Captain Mills interrupted his wayward subordinate. "Being a Winthrop does not allow you to subvert the orders of your Commanding Officer. Any Admiral Winthrop will tell you that." His expression changed from command to concern. "I cannot imagine the immense pressure you must be under, Mister Winthrop. Being the next Winthrop can't be an easy position to be in. The family name and their apparent expectations and your self-imposed expectations must be enough to confuse anyone. Right now your focus must not be on pleasing the Winthrops or becoming the next great Winthrop. Your focus must be dedicated to the *USS Card* and its welfare and the welfare of the crew. Be on board with me, or be gone."

"Sir . . ."

"Mister Winthrop I have a letter from you that stinks of mutiny. You would do well to keep silent now. You are dismissed. I advise you to leave the bridge while it is still your prerogative."

Mister Winthrop did an about face and left the bridge.

Later in the day Captain Mills sat in the wardroom reading Mister Goldsmith's plan. He noticed the Ensign had already plotted his progress on the Gantt chart. The plan was complete and very detailed.

Apparently Mister Goldsmith was no stranger to this type of assessment and renewal project. Mister Winchester's plan was lying just under Mister Goldsmith's. It also was complete and quite thorough.

XO McCormick had already reviewed it and marked several pages with yellow post-it notes. The captain was impressed with McCormick's notes regarding the areas he marked. It appears that Lieutenant Commander McCormick had some tutorials in this type of project. Anyway it was good to see his active involvement in the project.

Frank Hooper's report was incomplete. He had left a note paper-clipped to the cover that read; "not sure how detailed it needs to be in some areas. Will need the benefit of your thinking on those areas marked in the outline you gave us."

Mister Cavatini's report was not in the stack, but he had left a note on his spot on the Gantt chart that read; "I will need an hour of your time, Captain, to help with questions regarding the coordination between CIC and Radio Central. I stand ready at your convenience."

**Thursday Morning, 30 April 1970
USS Card Pier Side
US Coast Guard Yard, Curtis Bay, Maryland**

0900: The captain was in full dress white uniform when he stepped on the ship's quarterdeck. He was greeted by Lieutenant Grubaugh, the OOD and the Quarterdeck watch. The Quarter Deck watch keyed the 1-MC "*USS Card* arriving."

He had called ahead for Yeoman Williams to cut orders for Lieutenant Fridel. Williams stood up as the Captain entered his office. He slipped the file folder containing the paperwork into a large manila envelope and handed them to the Captain. "Shall I order you a good Engineering Officer Captain?"

No, Yeoman Williams, I ordered one from ComResDesRon. He will be here 14 June. This is someone I know well. He will be good for us. Call Mister Fridel and ask him to meet me in the wardroom."

When the Captain reached the wardroom Mister Fridel was there sipping a cup of coffee from a mug that displayed the ship's coat of arms on one side and the words *USS Card DE 383* on the other.

The captain handed the lieutenant the orders Williams had drawn up for him. "Lieutenant Fridel I am sending you to the Philadelphia Navy Ship Yard for further transfer to a duty station of your choice or retirement, which ever you choose."

"Won't you need me for the Gitmo battle operation?"

"No Mister Fridel. I have a car waiting to take you to the airport so if you will get your gear together you need be at the airport by 1200."

Mister Fridel was shocked, but in less than an hour he was in the car on his way to the airport.

The captain exited the wardroom and headed down the ladder leading to the "Oh-One" level. Chief Gruber was standing at the bottom of the ladder.

Captain Mills smiled and placed his hand on the chief's shoulder. "I know you heard about Mr. Fridel's decision to take early retirement."

"Yes sir, Mister Fridel chose a good time to retire."

"It looks like you will be running the engine room for this drill, and until 14 June when Mister Fridel's replacement will be arriving."

"Would that be Lieutenant Faulk. . . Captain?" "I know Lieutenant Faulk, sir. You could not have done better."

"Thank you chief, I concur. Carry on."

The Quarterdeck OOD informed the captain that Yeoman Williams needed to see him before he left the ship. "He said it was urgent and confidential."

The Captain met Yeoman Williams in the Administrative Office. "We found a spot for Mister Cavatini, Captain. Special Projects division, USNAVCOMMSTA Cheltenham, Maryland. I have the orders typed and ready for your signature."

"Excellent, Excellent! When you have a good employee but they can't do the job for which they were assigned you find a place where they can make a substantial contribution."

The captain signed the papers.

"He will receive his orders in the mail. He is to report there for his next reserve drill weekend," the Yeoman said.

"Give me the papers, Williams, I will deliver them myself. I don't want him to think we did not appreciate his situation."

The captain met with Lieutenant (jg) Cavatini at the *Warf* Restaurant at eleven hundred hours for lunch on Monday 06 April. They had just settled in when the waiter came for their drink orders. They ordered.

"This lunch is on me Mister Cavatini," The Captain began.

"The last time the boss took me to lunch I was being fired. Am I being fired Captain?"

"You are not being fired Lieutenant. You are being re-assigned. The reason I am giving you the word, instead of having you get a letter in the mail with new orders, is so you would not think you were being replaced because you were of no value. You are needed at the Special Project Division in the Naval Communications Station Cheltenham."

"That's big time!"

"It is big time. Your creative electronics skills will be a great value to that operation." The Captain placed an official looking envelop on the table and pushed it toward the officer. Mister Cavatini noticed the captain was carrying something when they first met in the lobby of the *Warf*, but took no more thought to it.

"Here are your orders. You are to report at your next drill weekend. You may, however make a visit before-hand in order to do some before reporting recon. The names of those you need to know are in here."

"I must say, this is a relief. I was very uncomfortable with the mess I found myself in, and frankly, I didn't know how I was going to clear all that up. You need a guy in there who has more management and organizational skills than I have."

'Well, that's all behind you now. This next assignment will be right in your ball park."

Chapter 7 Executive Assessment -Passing the Conn

Organizational Development

Getting the ship in combat shape is only one of the Captain's objectives. The other is developing a management team that can undertake all of the activities necessary to achieve the ship's mission. Only one person can bear the responsibility for bringing along a management team, and that is the chief executive. This is in fact one of the most important duties because the CEO is responsible for the continuity and survival of the organization. The job of subordinate executive development can be delegated of course and usually are, but the responsibility for the outcome remains with the CEO.

Effective uses of human resources are one of the four most important management responsibilities. The other three are production effectiveness, financial stability and strategic growth. This means creating an environment for individual opportunity. Support those who grasp it and replace those who do not. When considering the future of subordinate managers senior managers must consider the impact of the overall organization, not just the individual departments. For the health and continuity of the organization; anyone who does not contribute to that goal must be developed or replaced.

Maybe it was the "cold shower shock" of being stranded dead in the water that got the officer's attention. Maybe it was the humiliation of having to be rescued by the Coast Guard, maybe it was the Captain's tenacious hammering on the project and its mission or maybe it was abrupt adjournment of the meeting at the Warf when it was apparent the Captain was not going to show up. Maybe it was the crew eagerly identifying themselves with the ship after the captain had the ship's identification and coat of arms patches issued to the crew. Maybe it was the realignment of alliances when Cavatini, Grubaugh, Sterling and Goldsmith showed deliberate opposition to the Fridel, McCormick, and Winthrop cartel. Maybe word got back to the other officers that Mr. Winthrop came within a half hitch of being fired. Maybe it was all these reasons but they went to work on their assessments and organizational renewal (get-well) plans. Once the officers put their attention and skills to the task of getting their departments in place, they quickly realized they had the intelligence and competence to do what they had been told all this time, they could not do.

Mr. McCormick took the action the Captain had assigned to him. It looks as though he took the assignment seriously this time, as he applied his executive officer skills to the task of evaluating the plans and executing the approval process.

The Captain's "get well plan" is one aspect of a program called organizational development. O.D., according to Wendell French and Cecil Bell, is a top management supported long range effort to improve an organization's problem-solving and renewal processes. The process utilizes a thorough and effective collaborative diagnosis of management and the organization culture.

Special emphasis on formal work team, temporary team, and inter-group culture are also called for with the assistance of a consultant or facilitator and the use of the theory and technology of applied behavioral science, including action research and operational assessment. Captain Mills applied this method to the turn-around project, and served as the consultant, as well as the chief executive officer.

Organizational assessments, followed by a renewal program, were just what the officers and crew of the Card needed to get it back on track. Organizational renewal is the process of confronting current conditions and determining how those conditions either help or hinder the organization's operations. This is followed by a carefully controlled Organizational Renewal program consisting of initiating, creating, and confronting needed changes so as to make it possible for organizations to become or to remain viable, to adapt to new conditions, to solve problems, to learn from the experiences of those in the organization, in the hourly ranks as well as the management and executive ranks. The renewal process brings the results of change into line with purpose. Organizational Development guru Chris Argyris identifies organization renewal this way: "At the heart of organizational development is the concern for the vitalizing, energizing, activating, and renewing of organizations through technical and human resources".

The captain required each department head to make an assessment of their department. They were to begin with what they considered to be the mission of their area of responsibility and how it contributes to the overall mission of the USS Card and spell out, in detail, the action they must take to bring their department up to combat readiness. They were told to set priorities and work those priorities.

They were to compare their department's current condition with basic naval requirements, study the combat readiness exercise schedules that affect their department and develop a plan for meeting those objectives with specific goals, target dates and milestones for measuring progress. They were to meet with the members of their department and secure the benefit of their experiences when making up their plans. They were to establish plans for developing the necessary skills among their people with training plans and realistic exercises.

They were told to submit their plan to Mr. McCormick who would evaluate them and he and the captain would determine the resources, training and material needed to get their department ready for the GTMO experience.

The military provides detailed guidance on what needs to be operational, how maintenance is to be done, and how everything is to be operated. Very little is left to imagination. The officers need only to look at the Navy provided information to figure out their paths forward. My experience with strong, profitable organizations has had this same depth of documented procedures based on in-depth research and testing. Some executive teams, with whom I have worked, conduct an organizational renewal program every three to five years, as a prelude to their three to five year strategic planning process. They do this to avoid organizational decay and senility; the regaining of vitality, creativity, and innovation; the furtherance of flexibility and adaptability.

They claim this process, with the assistance of teams of hourly personnel, is the key to establishing conditions that encourage individual motivation, competency development and career fulfillment.

Rule of Command #12

The most significant factor of the manager's responsibility is creating an environment for individual opportunity. Reward those who embrace it, replace those who do not.

Management Axiom:

If you always do what you have always done you will always get what you always got. Is that what you want?

Never under-estimate the power of association. When one identifies with an organization they feel compelled to contribute to it. When one attacks their organization they see it as a personal attack against their person.

Training & Development

Isn't it interesting that "Training" pops up so often when exploring the concept of management? We saw how it influences organizational culture, Morale, Discipline, Motivation. It is axiomatic, then that managers should pay attention to training in their operation.

A Naval reserve vessel is required to conduct continuous training, to maintain the crew's combat readiness. In answering Mr. Hooper's question regarding the Card's current state of readiness Captain Mills said; "Mr. Hooper, our mission is to maintain a combat-ready US Naval warship, with a highly trained crew prepared to move and function effectively in a moment's notice, to engage the enemy and prevail, to practice for that mission one weekend each month and test that readiness each year with the squadron in Guantanamo Bay". The mission statement indicates that training is a significant aspect of the mission. Training should be included in the mission statement as a priority in any worthwhile enterprise."

Successful organizations in the world today are those staffed with competent personnel. Competence does not come by happenstance. Competency development is a deliberately planned and executed program of continuous training evaluation and development. Standards Based Training is training directed to the achievement of specific pre-established standards. Standards based training states precisely what the trainee must do (task) and the conditions under which the task must be performed and the training standard they must meet. Standards based competency development is not an event, it is a continuous process.

Standards based performance oriented trained personnel are expected to solve problems, participate in team efforts and generally, maintain a continuous learning process, to expand the scope of their role and competence. Performance appraisals should include training programs attended and the performance progression that resulted from that training.

Employees will learn without being trained, but they may not learn the job correctly. You have heard it said, all they have to do is get in and do it often enough and they will learn it. Well practice does not make perfect. Practice makes permanent! The most effective training is as a progressive competence development program, specifically directed to one's job classification that moves new employees from entry level (non competent) to competent, then from competent to subject matter expert in a significantly shorter time than conventional "plug n' play" methods.

Before one begins a training program it must first be determined if that person has the ability and the aptitude for the job. Ability is the capacity, mental and physical fitness to perform the required tasks. If ability is present then knowledge of the job can be learned and the needed skills can be developed.

I love golf. I very much enjoy the game. I have the knowledge, I learned that easy enough but I do not have the ability, the hand and eye coordination required to develop the skills needed to play it well. Knowledge is only one third of the competence needed to be good at something; there is also the ability to do the job and the skill to do it well. If the hiring process is geared to identify certain traits that identify a person's penchant for learning and the application of that learning,

A good "job fit" will almost ensure a competent long-term employee who will eventually be worth more than they are paid. The U.S. armed forces uses training and development and career development extensively and it has prepared men and women to take on jobs and activities that have history making or history saving consequences. The modern armed forces are made up largely of "children" the average age is 23 (2005 figures). Young men and women transitioning from high school or college are immediately placed in a comprehensive training program that proceeds from one element to another, according to their professional progression, but it is a situation that never ends until they leave the service. One of my friends was an officer on a nuclear submarine. He told me they had a crew of 14 officers and 130 enlisted. The average age of all crew members, including the C.O. was about 23. They carried the world's most lethal firepower, all manned by competent, and highly trained 20 somethings.

The military requires a structured, standardized, formalized series of training for each specific skill area. Training is geared toward operational conditions. Operations at sea are very hazardous every minute of every day. Much of the training is geared to handle actual combat conditions. They are required to test the operator's knowledge, skill and ability with written tests, and on-the-job activities. Civilian organizations could benefit by emulating the military's training structure by employing training that simulates actual on the job conditions, with skills competency testing.

The first step to any training program is to write an honest job description that is based on a job analysis and process analysis. The objective of any training program is to transfer learning, knowledge and skills to the trainee. Competency development requires a structured process that provides a progressive skills development over a specific period of time.

Regardless of the method used the training should provide physical and psychological fidelity. Physical fidelity is real world representation of equipment and psychological fidelity is real world representation of behavior and sense stimulation.

The lack of effective training will adversely affect the organization's ability to carry out its mission.

Progressive organizations today make the necessary investment in their skilled operators, technicians and professionals by providing the opportunity for competency development training programs at educational institutes technical update conferences at company expense. These investments serve to ensure they are able to maintain cutting edge operations in step with today's industrial market demands. I have heard executives ask; "What if we spend a lot of training dollars developing skilled people and they leave us?" To that I reply; "What happens if we don't train them and they stay?"

Again, consider the military. Many young people who enlist in the armed forces do not stay more than 4 years. A substantial amount of time and money is invested in them just for that short period of time, but it pays off with efficient competence on the job.

Training in job competence promotes self discipline in the skills application process but it also promotes self discipline in personal behavior and conduct. Too often organizations do not invest time and money in employees because they believe that after the initial training that brings them from entry level non competent to competent there is no further need to invest an expert's time or organization money for more advanced training. When an effectiveness measure is placed on the training a whole new meaning is added to competence training.

A major candy manufacturer was experiencing waste of over 6 batches of raw candy per day at 200 pounds per batch and a cost of forty eight cents per pound. The company decided that this problem may be solved by training since the development of a competency based training program required a job and process analysis. The job and process analysis revealed the problem began upstairs where the slurry was made. After experimenting with several methods of humidity and temperature control the problem was identified and solved. That was the end of the $576.00 per day waste. The water and sewer company charged this candy company $100,000 per quarter for handling all this waste.

Once the waste was gone, the one hundred-thousand dollar surcharge also disappeared.

As the training progressed the skill of the operators improved and the yield per batch improved so there was more candy to sell. The candy looked better and appeared to be more value for the money as a result of finding a better polishing technique.

The improved appearance improved sales by almost three-million dollars in six months after the training began. For a $30,000 investment the company realized a savings of $151,840.00 every three months for as long as the company continued to make that type of candy. As a direct result of training the sales department reported an increase of three million dollars in revenue every six months thereafter. The company also witnessed a decrease in accidents and lost time due to illness.

Once a company put a measurement to the effectiveness of a training system that's when they get serious about training. When a training system is put into place, the training manager should visit the company's controller and find out what is being measured or tracked and by whom and for what reason. Most production managers know how much a machine costs them sitting idle, and what it cost operating. They know how much a machine is capable of producing. This is just one small item to track.

A visit to the quality manager and the safety manager and the production control manager will provide other important items to measure against the training. The identified measures become the standard for measurement. It could be the measures from the first day the job analysis begins and or it could be measurements from the best day of the past year but whatever the time frame it becomes the base-line. These items are tracked everyday on a training effectiveness chart compared to the base-line. In every instance of my experience the numbers improved during the job and process analysis and skyrocketed once the best method was found and employed. In every instance the training had paid back the training investment long before the actual training actually begun, and exponentially thereafter.

Value measuring and training effectiveness measurements transform the training function from an overhead or cost center function to a self-sustaining function at least and a money maker at best. Training effectiveness measure will provide top management with evidence that the training operations' monetary and non-monetary value is greater than the resources expended to sustain it.

At the heart of the training effectiveness measuring project is the concern for the vitalizing, energizing, activating, and renewing the organization through technical and human resources.

Before getting underway all those involved in getting the ship away from the pier, through the channel and into the open sea rehearsed the operation until everyone knew their assignments and how to perform them. Nothing can be left to chance in any activity where production and safety are concerned.

Before any major activity is undertaken, particularly if it is a new process, a careful and detailed walk through should be made, and it should continue until everyone is satisfied the success of the actual activity is assured.

Management Axioms:

- Management is responsible for creating and maintaining a climate of success through a disciplined program of progressive training.

- To ensure an effective training system each activity must show how it can be measured in monetary and non-monetary values. Thus the training function is less an overhead function or cost center and more of a profit center.

- Practice does not make perfect. Practice makes permanent! The most effective method for assuring expected outcomes is to train for those outcomes. Practice it to meet the standards and test against those standards.

- Training is a morale booster and a cultural imperative. How can a company believe in quality and not believe in training.

The military consistently practices for events that may never happen, or may happen once in a lifetime. When that event occurs it must be done correctly the first time. There are many such situations in private industry. This develops a mindset. Be prepared, be expert, be flexible and act quickly.

Passing the Conn – Management Succession

Management succession simply refers to the process of preparing an organization for a transition in leadership. It is a critical factor in the strategic planning as a company must provide systems for finding personnel to fill its most important executive positions. It is an ongoing process of ensuring a suitable supply of successors for current and future senior or key positions arising from business strategy.

In addition to a structured training culture, effective organizations practically ensure their longevity through career development programs initiated by the company and paid for, in part or in whole, by the organization. Many firms are now engaging "career ladders" that assist employees to map their progression in a selected field and offer financial and career counseling support. Career development and "career ladders" include management succession, and professional position succession programs as well as tracking the evolution or growth of certain departments and professional positions within the company. To take advantage of the tracking system the company offers job bidding, internal transfer and promotion opportunities that follow a structured program of preparation for those "future" job opportunities.

Employees are more likely to stay with a company and give it their talent and commitment when they know it is that company that makes their success possible.

Captain Sorenson told Captain Mills of their plans to replace the *U.S.S. Card* with Fast Frigate and they will be in need of competent officers to serve on the management team and a commanding officer capable of delivering a well operating warship. We are talking about a highly technical warship. The new ship will be utilizing a technology far superior to those on the *Card*. Sophisticated high level technology in the propulsion systems, the communication systems and the weapons systems. Not just the officers but the professional crew will be required to have cutting edge technical skills in order to operate the sophisticated equipment used on board. This is not unlike what is happening in industry today. New technologies are being introduced every day in order to stay ahead of the market place. These new technologies necessitate the need for bringing in new people that have the skills to put these technologies to good use and for a continuous learning and training process for those in the hourly ranks and in the executive ranks. The Navy will send everyone to schools to learn what they need to learn.

Human Resources Planning is a process of anticipating and providing for the movement of people and specific competencies into, within, and out of the organization.

HRP is a formal system directed toward determining about how many and what types of people will be needed to conduct the work of the firm over a continuously sliding 60 day to three year time frame. It is a continuous examination of the nature of the business and determining when a position will be needed and what specific competencies are needed for that position.

Organizations must be constantly assessing the landscape to determine what will be expected in terms of what products and services to offer, either through development or acquisition. In what business do we expect to be in the next two to five years, and what does that mean in terms of what we do and where we do it. Included in the ongoing assessments are planning for future turnover. It includes an analysis of the various departments that make up the current management team and determining what if any of those departments will be doing in the near future, and again what skills will be needed by the department head.

The system includes predicting the turnover rate in each department and making provision for replacing them. Recruitment, selection and layoffs are part of the HRP activities required to attain the required number of employees. Planning for training and development to ensure the proper competencies and talent is part four of the planning process. It is imperative that senior management include human resources executives, skilled in HRP and succession planning in the strategic planning process.

The assessments must also focus on the management and professional skills that will be required to ensure successful competition in the marketplace. Management succession planning is as critical if not more critical than competency and technical skills assessment.

Executive succession planning involves a periodical review of top executives and those in the lower management levels to determine who of them may be suitable backups for each senior management position. If potential candidates show promise the company's management team in concert with the training staff should be geared to bring them up to speed, through mentoring, training, job rotation and special assignments directed toward developing certain skills needed for the position for which they are being groomed.

If the production of the incumbent is not likely to meet anticipated requirements for the next fiscal year, a program of competency improvement may be helpful or action should be taken for securing a replacement must begin.

If the needed talent is not expected to be present within the current management ranks, the HR people involved in the strategic planning must make plans to recruit for this talent from outside the organization.

The key to successful management succession planning is preparing a written succession plan. This document provides a road map for determining when department head and executive positions are expected to become vacant for any number of reasons and set a time frame and a program for grooming a successor to fill the vacant spots. The assessment should also project the skills needed in this position that may be different from what is now required. Duties and task change and those changes are to be reflected and include that in the successor selection process.

Most importantly is the position of the top executives, the CEO, the Chairman of the Board, the Chief Operating Officer, Chief Financial Officer and the like. A succession committee should be actively planning the careers of individuals and managing to optimize the organization's needs and the individual's aspirations. I recommend that boards of directors meet at least two times each Fiscal Year to discuss the issue of CEO succession. The CEO succession issue should be a major part of a larger, formal written Human Resources manpower planning program.

Management Axiom

Employees are more likely to stay with a company and give it their talent and commitment when they know it is that company that makes their success possible.

Management Axiom:
More often than not managers will not jump ship when they know the organization is not only clearing a spot for them higher up but is paying for the opportunity

When people realize they have greater abilities, and consequent confidence because of the programmed career ladder they will most likely stay with it and see how far they can go in the organization.

Evaluating the Performance of Subordinate Managers.

Performance appraisal is a systematic process of monitoring, evaluating and matching an individual employee's on-the-job performance with pre-established performance standards set for the job they are performing. This will help ensure consistent adherence to those standards and adjusting the standards or work assignments as necessary to meet the changing needs of the organization. First there must be a description of the responsibilities assigned to the job, then a detail description of the duties that are performed in order to meet those responsibilities. Each responsibility must have a measurable outcome, and each duty must have established standards of performance, conduct, quality, quantity, etc., that allow the job holder to first measure themselves against those standards so they can make corrections before the job holder's supervisor does officially.

Performance appraisal has a significant place in each member's tenure in the organization and their career.

An honest appraisal that actually measures performance provides the information needed for discovering training required to bring them to the standards or to exceed the standards. An honest appraisal will tell us, over time, if indeed that person can do the job, or can learn to perform at higher levels. If the performance appraisal reveals inability to do the job, and an inability to grow into it within a reasonable period of time that member must be replaced by someone who can. Each person in the organization must be exponentially worth more than they are paid.

There are several factors to consider when evaluating the performance of senior management personnel. The key technical requirements for the position the executive now holds and should show evidence that indicates if that technical competence is effective or needs improvement. The appraisal instrument should include evidence of management competence in the areas of planning, organizing, directing and controlling. Consider the projects the executive undertaken in the past fiscal year the effectiveness of the outcomes. The instrument should explore the next position this executive could be moved into. It should explore the technical and management skills displayed and the contribution to the organization during the target time frame.

In determining the fate of the officers on the USS Card, and to determine if they should be the management team for the GTMO exercises there are certain things we need to consider:

Does the manager possess the management and technical skills needed to make a contribution to the organization in this exercise?

Does the manager have the attitude and the culture to succeed in this endeavor? Can this officer be brought up to competence in time for the GTMO cruise? (When considering managers for your organization you want to know if they can be brought up to speed in time to meet some major organizational goal.)

What will be the impact of your decision on their department and the organization? What is this executive's career needs? Will this project satisfy those needs?

Let's appraise the performance of the officers on the USS Card.

Lieutenant Commander McCormick: He has the management and technical skills needed to make a contribution to the organization. He would be more effective if we sent him to Command and Control School. Pay attention to his assigned portion of the "Get Well Plan." Help him understand the what, and the why of the assessments. Mister McCormick has experience, not just time in grade. He knows the ship and the responsibilities that go with the job so we need to bring Mr. McCormick with us to the GTMO exercises. His professional needs and personal self-worth would be greatly enhanced with the exercise. When Mister McCormick is removed from the shadow of Mr. Winthrop and the legacy of Captain Gallagher he performed honorably.

His credibility with the crew will return. The question that needs to be asked has to do with whether Mr. McCormick has the skills for assignment to the Fast Frigate when it arrives.

An assessment of the talent and skills needed at his level for the Frigate and Mr. McCormick's ability and aptitude for skills development will tell the tale. The Navy has a good management succession plan that will not leave the Frigate without competent executives.

Lieutenants Grubaugh and Sterling, and Lieutenant (j.g.) Cavatini are effective officers, who did not challenge the authority of Mr. McCormick and Mr. Winthrop but did their jobs and held their own. They will move up. Ms. Grubaugh deserves to be in a position of prominence the first time the ship makes its first successful run. They possess the management and technical skills needed to make a contribution to the organization.

They have good judgment and the required skills. The officers' career needs will be greatly benefited from the GTMO project. The Lieutenants are competent to handle the Frigate's needs, and the aptitude for any additional training to prepare her for the move.

Lieutenant (j.g.) Hooper and Ensign Winchester gave in to the leadership quagmire and went into the captain's program kicking and screaming. They are young and inexperienced; they must be unlearned and retrained. They can get that from this ship and its current leadership. They are bright persons and with some additional training and responsible leadership experience they will be very good officers. The officers' career needs will be greatly benefited from the GTMO project. They will move to the Frigate with additional competency upgrading.

Ensign Cavatini He was what consultants call a natural lieutenant. He was an excellent subordinate manager, an excellent technician, but he was not a leader. Mister Cavatini knew it was a position he knew was appropriate for him and was accepted with grace and loyalty. There is no doubt that he is a technically competent communications professional.

The questions that need an answer is whether his lack of organization and his apparent inability to apply any leadership or management activity to the radio central function will hamper operations when the ship enters the combat readiness competition. He was the right man for the job when technical skills, on that level, were needed to prepare for the big show. But when the ship goes to sea and enters the demands of combat a different set of skills will be needed.

Ensign Goldsmith is a competent supply and Human Resources officer. His problem is that he does not know how to delegate. He also needs training for creating political alliances, and how to exercise authority. He will stay and go to GTMO. He needs more management training and experience. He will be very valuable to the ship and ship's company at GTMO and beyond. This officer's career needs will be greatly benefited from the GTMO project. He will qualify for the Frigate.

Lieutenant Fridel Is one of those people, who can influence others, but he is an instigator and a demoralizer more than one who encourages. His suggestions are self-serving and not in the best interest of the organization or his fellow officers.

He has instigated a number of situations where another officer took the lead for one Mr. Fridel's bad ideas and was left taking the consequences for its failure. The meeting was Mr. Fridel's idea, and although Mr. Winthrop should have known better, he took the bullet for it. Mr. Fridel has not stayed up with the technology of the modern naval vessel's engine room. No doubt you know several Mister Fridels. The *USS Card* would be better off if Mr. Fridel did not go with them to GTMO. The Captain will send him to NavBase for early retirement. He needs to be replaced by a competent engineering officer.

Lieutenant Winthrop: Consider the pressure Mr. Winthrop has been under his entire life. When he received his ultimatum from the captain to get on board or get out, he told the captain he has been grooming for command since he was five years old. All his Navy Admiral family has high expectations of him and as a consequence has made great demands on him.

He had not done well in the Naval Academy. He was immediately sent to advance Naval warfare schools and then two shortened tours of duty on destroyers before being sent to the Card as OIC on a "Fast-track-to command" mandate with very little management or executive experience. If that was not pressure enough Captain Gallagher was suppose to disciple him but both Captain Gallagher and Lieutenant Commander McCormick surrendered command and took on no mentoring duties.

He had to pretend he knew he knew what he was doing. Mr. Winthrop is a narcissist with an unrealistic opinion of his own importance but he is smart, he is capable of influencing others, he has connections and he has the persistence to be a good officer and a good commanding officer. He is worth saving. He needs a frightening career threatening event. He needs a circumstance where preparation would be required and his decisions will be the central theme, one in which his credibility will be on the line.

When he falters, and he will falter, He will realize his dependence on the legitimate one in command. Captain Mills should begin mentoring him for future executive responsibilities.

He will go to GTMO. With some additional training and experiential assignments he will be very valuable to the ship and ship's company at GTMO and beyond. This officer's career needs will be greatly benefited from the GTMO project. Mr. Winthrop will no doubt be assigned to another ship in the fleet before the Frigate arrives.

Before we leave the topic of performance appraisal lets discuss the performance of the crew during the failed mission to get to the open sea. Lieutenants Winthrop and Fridel expressed the opinion that the "dead in the water" experience garnered more demoralization for the crew to the point they were no longer willing to continue with the preparations.

They said it took the heart right out of everyone on the ship. It may have been a great disappointment to them, but consider General Eisenhower's statement about morale.

He said it can withstand shocks and disasters on the battle field, but can be totally destroyed by neglect, favoritism and injustice. They actually got the ship underway something they had not done in two years, and some on that ship had never done.

The problem that caused the loss of all power had very little to do competence. Most of those on the ship did their jobs well. And to the enginemen the problem was mostly an equipment problem. While the lack of training was felt in some areas, it was not incompetence that caused the situation. It was a shock and a disaster but it was not demoralizing.

With regard to favoritism, neglect and injustice, they saw favoritism disappearing with the new captains command style, the injustice they suffered because of the ship's reputation and inability to make a contribution had been turned around, and they no longer felt neglected. A manager must recognize the difference between demoralization and disappointment. Disappointment can be cured by a realistic assessment of what went wrong and get them involved in fixing it.

The officers need to muster their people and assure them that this was a disappointment but look at what we actually accomplished. There will be a next time, and the next time we will make it.

Handling Executives Who Are No Longer Effective

Managers are measured by results, not activities, not hard work, not time in grade. Time in grade is not the same as experience. I know many managers and workers who have 10 years time in grade and they only have 6 months experience 20 times. These people never learn from situations that occur and never learn how to pro-act or innovate. Then there are those who were once competent and commanded respect but are no longer effective. In the Navy these people are called *ROAD-ies*, Retired On Active Duty.

They present a drain on the organization, not only in terms of poor departmental performance, but also in lost morale and upper management credibility. I once heard a junior executive say: I am not so upset by the fact that my boss is incompetent and ineffective, "I am more upset by the fact that upper management thinks he is competent."

How does one manage a situation where we have a subordinate manager that is no longer effective? We manage the situation as nature does. We show neither malice nor pity. Many managers face the cold-blooded reality of when an employee is not able to perform, or refuses to perform according to the pre-established standard. The situation is bad enough when the employee has always been incompetent, but it is worse when the subordinate has been a loyal, hard worker, but now is unable to do the job according to the performance standards.

Usually this situation does not come on us overnight. We can see it coming and the employee can see it coming.

Sometimes we tend to overlook poor performance, especially if the employee is in a low level position. Competent managers must not overlook performance problems at any level because disgruntled people at any level can cause havoc in the work unit.

Another reason many supervisors overlook the problem is they are unwilling to face the pain of confronting the poor performer. Many executives are reluctant to replace those who are no longer effective. Let's face it, telling someone that they are not getting the job done is not pleasant and having to fire someone ruins your entire afternoon.

Subordinate executives who have the ability to be effective but are not living up to their capabilities must be dealt with head on. The senior manager does not grant pity or inflict malice. The senior manager helps them to get an understanding of the mission and helps them get a plan for meeting expected objectives.

With regard to managers that have not been producing; get to the point right away. Do not keep them in suspense. Tell them in no uncertain terms they are not making the contribution they should be making in their present position.

State clearly what is expected. Warn poor performers. It is unwise to assume that anyone, even the veteran knows exactly what constitutes effective performance in your eyes. You may assume that subordinate managers know when their performance is unsatisfactory, but that is not often the case. Furthermore, subordinate managers deserve to have specific deficiencies spelled out. Make it clear what the consequences will be if improvement is not in evidence by a specific deadline. Spell out, in writing, the standards and goals, and your expectations so that they will clearly understand.

Set up a Work Improvement Plan. Provide an assignment that will require them to demonstrate their management and technical skills. Help them set up a plan and time frames. Check in with them regularly.

Evaluate their progress. Allow a reasonable period of time for improvement. During this time, require sub-par performers to raise performance and do what you can do to provide specific guidance and opportunities to acquire or sharpen the requisite skills.

I have terminated several people in my career but I actually fired only three. With the others who were terminated under my authority I just kept score and did the paperwork, they fired themselves. Among those I actually fired, two people committed an egregious act against the company. I prosecuted one and the other made a deal.

You must follow the policies and procedures regarding termination, of course. Before termination consider other options. If improvement is not coming along as quickly as needed have other options ready to consider. Assess their skills and look at potential openings that may be filled on a permanent basis. Temporary assignments only postpone the inevitable.

Explore the possibility of reassignment with additional training. If reassignment appears to be the best option, be sure it is a position that will provide them opportunities to make a substantial contribution. If all else fails terminate. If there is little or no improvement during this period, and other options are not practical, a notice of termination should be given.

You must remove the ineffective manager; even if you do not have a replacement for them.

But you might ask; "don't we owe the employee something?" After all they came to work here and they look to the company to provide a needed paycheck.

The senior manager owes the employee the right to know where they stand, with regard to the performance expectations of the department and how they measure up. But, remember this: You do not owe anyone a job, they can't handle.

If you hesitate at the unpleasant task of dealing with an incompetent employee, ask yourself: "How fair am I being to everyone else in the department who are doing their jobs?" "How fair am I being to the employee, who struggles every day, trying to do something they cannot do, and who is wondering when the ax will fall?"

If someone is ineffective or incompetent, or so hostile that no one wants to work with them, get them out of there. You do not owe anyone a job they can't handle or won't handle. You do not owe anyone a job if they refuse to maintain the standards. The other employees who must suffer with this person, or correct their mistakes, will appreciate the decision to remove the problem. To allow them to stay is to reward this behavior, and signals that organizational standards and values are not really important after all. When a person is no longer effective, and they cannot be transferred where they can make a substantial contribution to the organization they need to be discharged even if you don't have a replacement. It is better to leave a position vacant than to give it to someone who cannot handle it or who just will not fit in.

And don't think your organization's policies make it impossible to fire someone for poor performance or acts of disgrace against the company. I have worked with many of those organizations and I can tell you, as one of the senior executives told me; "Give me six months and I can fire the Pope!"

Rule of Command #13:

You do not owe anyone a job, they can't handle. It is better to leave a position vacant than to give it to someone who cannot handle it or who just will not fit in.

Chapter 8 Steady As She Goes

Saturday, 09 May
USS Card
Curtis Bay, Maryland to the Chesapeake Bay

The ship was alive with sailors anxious to get underway. There is always excitement and anticipation as the time nears. The regulation plan of the day (RPOD) called for getting underway at zero-nine hundred.

0730: The auxiliary and shipboard utilities engines were lit off and stabilized.

0800: The call was made to shift from shore power to ship power. The shift was made at zero eight-eleven (0811) without a glitch.

0820: The Boatswain keyed the 1-MC (ship-wide address system) and made an announcement that sent chills up the spine of the entire ship's company. They had heard it before, but this time was different. This time there was no doubt as to whether they could actually do it!

"Now . . . all hands . . . make preparation for getting underway."

0830: The second preparation announcement was made. "Now . . . set the special sea and anchor detail. The maneuvering watch will lay to the bridge."

0840: The third preparation announcement was made. "Now . . .The Officer of the Deck has shifted the watch from the quarterdeck to the flying bridge."

0855: The final getting underway order was given.

"Now . . . cast off all lines."

The lines were cast off from the pier and retrieved by the deck hands on the *Card*. They were promptly and properly coiled and placed in their proper storage space.

When the last mooring line was dropped and the Boatswain Mate of the Watch blew a long whistle blast and passed the word to shift colors. The jack and ensign were hauled down smartly and the *steaming* ensign was hoisted on the gaff and the ship's call sign was hoisted.

0900: The *Card* slipped easily away from the pier with no outside assistance and headed toward the channel that would lead them out to the open sea. They were followed by two fleet tugs dispatched by NavBase, .just in case.

The crew held their collective breaths. They made it this far the last time they tried to get out to sea, but didn't make it past the channel. The verbal exchanges between the crews of the ship and the fleet tugs were terse and professional.

Captain Mills sat in his chair on the Port side of the bridge. As before, Commander McCormick left his chair vacant to join, Lieutenant Sterling, the Officer of the Day observing the bridge's work stations.

There is a sea-going chart room just off the pilot house, but Captain Mills chose to utilize the chart table, securely anchored to the deck in the center of the bridge and to the rear right of the Captain's seat. Mister Winthrop was functioning as the Navigator, and was standing by the chart table.

Lieutenant Grubaugh had the Conn standing in front of the instrument panel and the windscreen. She responded to the responsibility of commanding a ship as naval officers always have. Standing erect and proud, she spoke the orders into the intercom. "Engine Room, Bridge. All ahead one third"

As the fleet tugs turned away, leaving the *Card* on her own there began a series of radio exchanges with the Harbormaster. The ship was being advised that an accident had occurred just around the bend from Hamilton Point. Two barges had broken loose from their tow, had collided and were now blocking the main shipping channel.

The auxiliary channel was quite narrow and generally shallower than the main channel. There was a risk involved, but the captain determined it was important to get the *Card* out to sea. Another 'turn back' might be too much for the crew's fragile morale.

"Mister Winthrop, give us a heading for the auxiliary channel," the captain ordered.

Lieutenant Grubaugh turned her head so she could see if the captain was serious about going into the auxiliary channel. She did not say anything.

Mister Winthrop spoke up. "Sir, I have been in the auxiliary channel and it is very narrow and shallow."

"I am aware of that Mr. Winthrop. A heading if you please."

Mister Winthrop breathed out a sigh, but very low, as to not appear to challenge the order. He looked at his charts.

"Perhaps we should seek permission from the Harbormaster before entering the auxiliary channel, Captain."

The captain spun around in his swivel seat and looked directly at Mister Winthrop. There was no anger in his expression or his tone but there was no question about his resolve.

"The Harbormaster is not in command of this ship, Mister Winthrop. Lieutenant Grubaugh needs a heading."

"Three – two – five. . . . dead slow. *Sir.*"

The Captain looked toward Lieutenant Grubaugh. "Three – two - five. . . Slow," the captain repeated.

Grubaugh pressed the intercom: "Helmsman, left standard rudder; steady on course Three – two - five."

The intercom responded: "Helmsman. . . . Left standard rudder; steady on course Three – two - five. Aye."

The Ship turned and headed into the auxiliary channel as all hands held their breath. Expressions on faces indicated there was deep concern about the Captain's decision to take this route. No one spoke of it aloud.

The Conn Lieutenant keyed the intercom again. "Engine room."

"Engine room Aye."

"Engine room all head slow if you please."

"All ahead slow . . . Aye."

Navigator Lieutenant Winthrop had been furiously working on the chart of the ship channels since the exchange with the Harbormaster. Now he spoke across the bridge to the captain.

"Sir, I don't believe we should attempt the auxiliary ship channel. It's much too shallow and we'd be in danger of running aground."

The captain continued to look straight ahead. "Steady as she goes," he intoned.

The ship continued on its course, gliding, slowly but smoothly through the water. All hands on the bridge tried to concentrate on the chores of their duty station but all kept stealing furtive glances at the approaching buoy markers, showing the entrance to the auxiliary channel.

"Captain," the Navigator spoke again, his voice a note higher this time. "I strongly recommend we bare a course of one eight zero, and that we heave-to and wait for further information of the main channel."

"Steady as she goes. . . Mr. Winthrop," was the captain's only response.

Another few moments passed. They were entering the auxiliary channel now. Navigator Winthrop's voice seemed almost pleading. "Sir, I'm reading the charts, and they indicate we're in danger of running aground!"

Captain Mills was still impassive. "I've read the charts myself, Mister Winthrop. Lieutenant Grubaugh has been given a heading of Three – two – five, a speed of all ahead slow and steady."

Seconds ticked off on the Chelsea clock. Mister Winthrop was unable to contain himself.

"Sonar," he spoke into his intercom, "I want constant readouts from the fathometer."

The Captain turned and looked in the direction of Lieutenant Winthrop. He said nothing and his expression did not change. Then he turned back forward and took a sip from his coffee cup and continued his attention to the ships forward progress.

Lieutenant Commander McCormick and Mister Winthrop exchanged glances but said nothing. Their facial expressions gave away their thoughts.

"He had us convinced he knew what he was doing, but how do you explain this unconscionable decision?"

Lieutenants Grubaugh and Sterling continued to stare ahead trying to ignore what was taking place.

"Sonar, Aye," came the response over the loudspeaker. "Reading one zero...one zero...one zero..." it continued to read, giving the water's depth in six-foot increments. "Zero nine," it changed. "Zero six," it changed again. Zero five...Zero five...Zero five...Zero four...Zero four...Zero four..."

"Captain," a voice on the bridge broke in, "after-watch reports we're churning mud astern."

"Captain," Winthrop's voice repeated, "we're churning mud. I recommend we reverse engines and bear a course of zero – five - five."

"My order was steady as she goes." Captain Mills turned to his right, picked up his cup of coffee, took a sip and looked into the cup. Leaning forward he flipped a switch on his intercom and spoke into it.

"Galley, this is the Captain. Please have a Commissaryman bring up some fresh coffee."

Winthrop was stunned. "Captain, may I have it entered in the log that at zero nine forty, Navigator, Lieutenant Winthrop, requested we reverse engines and bear zero – five - five and it was denied by the Captain?"

Captain Mills turned toward Mister Winthrop, and in a matter-of fact tone asked "Is that what you want to do Mister Winthrop?"

"'Indeed Captain, I do."

"Very well," The Captain turned toward the windscreen. "Enter it in the log, Quartermaster . . . steady as she goes Lieutenant Grubaugh."

The loudspeaker had continued its monotone. "Zero three...zero three...zero four...zero four..."

Ten minutes went by, for those on the bridge it seemed like an hour. The captain's steward entered the bridge with a thermos of coffee. He took the Captain's cup and filled it.

"Thank you Baker, you may take the thermos."

"Aye Sir," the steward turned and disappeared down the ladder.

The Captain took of sip of coffee, and propped his feet up on the ledge in front of his big chair.

Another fifteen minutes passed as the ship continued to glide slowly through the water and the Sonarman continued the monotonous soundings over the intercom. They arrived at mid-point on the auxiliary channel. The crew members on the bridge were now craning their necks, looking at the buoys which marked their re-entry point into the main channel.

"Zero five... zero five...one zero..."

The captain seemed to be the white elephant in the room as he just sat relaxed in his chair, his legs propped up on the ledge, sipping his coffee and peering out on the channel ahead.

Lieutenant Winthrop was no longer looking at the charts on the table in front of him, He had moved to the windscreen beside Mr. McCormick. He stood with his face only inches from the windscreen of the bridge; transfixed on the surface of the auxiliary channel which was rapidly being put behind the ship.

"Lieutenant, the after-watch reports clear wake, no mud astern," shouted the starboard watch standing outside the flying bridge area.

"Two one . . . .two five . . . two five . . . two niner . . . three zero...three zero..."

"Belay the fathometer reports." There was huskiness in Winthrop's voice as he spoke into the intercom.

"Sonar, Aye."

The *Card* approached and then passed the marker buoys as they gained the edge of the main channel.

The bridge was silent except for the crackle of radio traffic in the background. The ship moved smoothly down the channel, cutting through the increasingly larger waves. Every sailor not at a fixed station found a way to look outside. They watched Parrot Head Island slip away to starboard; they were now in the main channel. Every sailor on board felt a surge of pride, they realized they had succeeded. The *Card* . . . was at sea.

Mister Winthrop was still standing with his face by the windscreen as he spoke. "Captain, may I have it entered in the log that at ten thirty hours, Navigator, Lieutenant Winthrop, conveyed his apologies to the Captain for his attitude and conduct toward the Captain?"

Captain Mills looked straight ahead, and asked, "Is that what you want to do Mr. Winthrop?"

"Yes Captain, it is."

Captain Mills continued to look straight ahead as he spoke. "Very well . . . enter it in the log, Quartermaster."

Navigator Winthrop moved to the Navigator's table and found the chart of the area they had entered.

Captain Mills eased out of his chair and walked over to the Navigator's table. He leaned in, close to the Lieutenant's ear, put his hand on his forearm, and spoke to him in a low tone. "They re-dredged the auxiliary ship channel last January Mister Winthrop. It is shallow but it will accommodate a ship of our size. I verified the soundings with the Harbormaster, myself, just yesterday. A responsible navigator would have done the same."

The Captain then moved to the rear of the bridge and gazed over the weather decks, over the oh-three level, past the stack, past the fantail and into the bubbling wake generated by a ship . . . at sea. He took a sip from his coffee cup, and held it in both hands as he surveyed the deck crew at work. He took a mental note of the sailors on the bridge diligently focusing on the work required of competent maritime professionals . . . on a U. S. Navy ship . . . at sea.

The captain turned his attention to Lieutenant Grubaugh.

"All ahead one third, Lieutenant Grubaugh."

"All ahead one third Captain. . . Aye."

She keyed the intercom. "Engine room . . . all ahead one third."

"Engine room all ahead one third . . . Aye."

The captain turned toward the navigator who was focusing on the charts, more as a way of hiding his face, than studying their position. "And now Navigator Lieutenant Winthrop." He was using his command voice again.

Mister Winthrop looked up at the Captain, with a look of dread. He had suffered enough humiliating events this morning, what was next?

"What course do you recommend?" asked Captain Mills, smiling.

Mister Winthrop consulted the chart one more time just to make certain, but he had already charted the course and knew the coordinates.

"Captain, I recommend a heading of zero niner zero in sixty-seconds."

Commander Mills turned and looked in the direction of Lieutenant Grubaugh who was standing in command position looking forward. "Zero niner zero you say?" still looking in the direction of the Lieutenant Grubaugh who had the conn.

"Zero niner zero," Lieutenant Winthrop repeated.

"Thank you Mister Winthrop." He said still looking in the direction of Lieutenant Grubaugh. "And now Lieutenant Grubaugh, let's see what this "old bucket" can do, what-a-ya say?"

"You mean this magnificent vessel, Captain?" she responded. "I say let's go for it."

The captain almost smiled. "This . . . magnificent vessel . . . Lieutenant Grubaugh . . . was designed to do 24 knots. Let's see if she still has it in her. We will go to two-thirds, hold her steady for five minutes, long enough for her to catch her breath, then go to all ahead full for 20 minutes, then flank for 20 minutes. Let see what her top out looks like. Then back to two-thirds for 20 minutes, then take her down to one third and hold her steady. We'll cruise there for an hour or so then Mister McCormick will take his turn."

"Aye, Aye, Sir." She turned and keyed the Intercom. "Helmsman this is the bridge."

"Helm Aye".

"Come right to zero niner zero and steady as she goes."

"Helmsman right zero niner zero and ...steady... as she . . . **goes** . . . aye." (The Helmsman emphasized goes).

The ship turned into the wind and continued its forward progression.

She keyed the intercom again. "Engine room this is the bridge."

"Engine Room, Aye."

"This is the bridge **. . . all ahead** . . . two-thirds." (She emphasized all ahead).

"Engine Room **all ahead** . . . **two thirds** aye." (The engineman emphasized all ahead and a greater emphasis on two thirds.) There was a smile in his voice.

The ship surged forward and with increasing speed she knifed through the ocean swells quickly increasing in speed. The big diesel engines created a gentle vibration but the *Card* was moving fast and moving well.

The captain moved once more to the navigation charts, where Mister Winthrop was busying himself tracking the movement. He bent over the charts beside him, their shoulders touching. They were both looking down at the chart. In the same low tone he used before he said; "In the future, Mister Winthrop, I expect you, as Navigator, to be better prepared."

Mister Winthrop leaning against his elbows on the chart shifted his face slightly left facing the Captain. "In the future? . . . Sir?" His expression was one of reserved surprise.

"Beginning now. . . Mister Winthrop."

"Yes Sir."

"Are we square . . . Mr. Winthrop?"

With his eyes were focused on the chart he answered. "I am yours to command Captain." He turned his face toward the Captain his expression revealed that he really meant it. He had met his match, the best man won He realized his career had been saved.

"Very well then." The captain straightened up to his command height and patted his OIC twice in rapid succession on the shoulder. In his command voice he said; "Carry on Lieutenant."

He turned back to the center of the bridge. Mister McCormick you will see that all the officers are qualified at the Conn."

"Aye Aye Sir."

In his command voice now he declared, "Lieutenant Grubaugh, you have the Conn. I'll be in CIC." Captain Mills entered the starboard companion way and disappeared down the ladder toward the Combat Information Center. The Duty Boatswain's mate bark into the ship's intercom system reverberated throughout the ship.

"The Captain is off the bridge."

Five minutes had clicked off the Chelsea clock and Lieutenant Grubaugh once again keyed the mike. "Engine Room - bridge."
"Engine Room Aye."

"All ahead full."

"All ahead full Aye, Aye."

As the warship surged forward, the giant starboard Cummins Diesel and the port Detroit Diesel sent loud vibrations through the ship, but the vessel was up to the task and charged headlong into the swells.

"Engines answer all ahead full indicating 60 revolutions for 18 knots bridge."

"Very well."

She stared straight ahead, at the bow of the ship skimming through the swells she clenched her teeth and fought back a welling up of tears. In her entire life, she couldn't remember feeling as happy, or proud as she did at this moment. She turned to look at Lieutenant Sterling. She had a proud look and tears also. They smiled at each other, each knowing they had made the right decisions and they shared in the success. Without saying a word they faced forward again.

The starboard watch standing on the balcony outside the flying bridge area keyed the mike on the sound-powered phone strapped to his chest. His voice was only heard by the other weather deck watches stationed at various strategic intervals around the ship.

"Well what a-ya know, the old man pulled it off!"

"Roger that" chimed in the forward watch.

Mister Winthrop muttered something under his breath. The entire quarterdeck compliment heard it but couldn't be sure they heard it right.

"What's that you say Mister Winthrop?" Mister McCormick inquired.

"I said we may be on a fool's errand, but blast it all, we just may be a magnificent bunch of fools."

"Aye. . . That we be, Mister Winthrop." replied the Executive Officer in his best Long John Silver impression, "That we be."

Chapter 8 Assessment - Steady As She Goes

Learning at the Feet of the Masters

There actually was a collision in the main channel that led from the Coast Guard Yard to the open sea, but whether the radio traffic claiming that to be the situation actually said the channel was blocked forcing the *Card* to use the auxiliary channel we will never know. There was a rumor going around that Captain Mills and the Harbor Master created that scenario in order to reveal Mr. Winthrop's unrealistic image. If he had the good sense of the officer he has potential of becoming, he would see the captain gave him a chance to redeem himself and get with the program. In any case, the captain had figured Mr. Winthrop right and he knew his Navigator would not have done his homework and prepared for any contingencies and alternative plans for getting out to sea. It was an opportunity for Mr. Winthrop to show his true colors. The captain has had experience with people like John Winthrop. The barge collision worked in the Captain's favor, as did the recent dredging of the auxiliary channel.

Captain Mills visited with the Harbor master to work out contingencies in order to avoid another botched launch. He was almost certain the ship was sea worthy and could make it to the open sea, function effectively and return. He was certain the crew had been trained well enough to stay out for the weekend. He now had to make sure he, and those officers who would be standing command duty would not run aground or experience some other unexpected mishap. He checked the charts with the harbor master and even took a cruise through both channels with a coast guard patrol boat.

Mister Winthrop had been a thorn in the Captain's side from the time he came on board. He was belligerent, independent and bordered on disrespectful but at least he had the good sense to refrain from being insubordinate. He had an unrealistic perception of leadership, management and command that was handed down from his previous commander who had abdicated the command mantel and given it to one whom he knew would make his few remaining years comfortable without any real challenges. What was worse he had a reputation for being a "king maker,"

Consequently the Winthrop naval dynasty relied on Footsellers Gallagher to do for the next generation of Winthrops what he had done for so many other Naval Academy protégés. But instead of passing on his great wisdom, leadership and command philosophies he allowed Mr. Winthrop develop his own based on what he observed at the feet of the legendary naval guru. Combine that with the serpent advice from Lieutenant Fridel, absence of any demonstrated experience from Lieutenant Commander McCormick, and the entire Officer-in-charge program had been detrimental to the *USS Card* as an entity and to the officers and crew that manned her. This is a good lesson to the chief decision makers for family owned businesses and to those owners of closely-held private corporations.

Be careful who you entrust to develop the future leaders of the business. Monitor closely what is being passed down. Make sure the chosen are being taught the values and principles you want the organization to follow. I have more respect for personal maturity and professional competence than I do for education or publication. Trust the one who can provide the opportunity for experiencing exhilaration of mastering a job, can actually provide the means for one to motivate toward some daily accomplishment that comes from worthwhile work. Worthwhile work in an operation that holds itself and its employees to standards that will ensure a healthy organization.

With regard to leadership, so often the masters' definition of leadership is vague, or it orders the sharing of command, or giving away the ship to those who have not earned either the right or the ability to carry the custodial mantel. When mentoring candidates for executive responsibilities one must not neglect the elements of stewardship and command, the significance of the organization as the goose that lays the golden eggs, the entity that houses the opportunities for everyone employed to experience life in the microcosm of the work place. If the decisions you make are for the good of the organization they will be good for the people employed by it.

Trust those who know the benefits individuals garner from working in a place that provides the arena to witness and experience order, structure, self respect, a worthwhile task, a chance to develop a marketable skill. The well managed organization offers security, a social status, of friends and co-workers. I was amazed to learn how many people escape life by coming to work in a disciplined operation where they know what they are doing and have some control over what is going on.

In business and in life one can only enjoy living in a culture if they have the opportunity to learn and grow and apply their skills to a worthwhile task, and witness failure without being defeated, witness success without developing the notion that your way is the only right way. There are risks and set-backs, there are successes and each of them contributes to our sense of self. Where would man-kind be if there was no work, no situation in which we could be challenged and strengthened?

I know executives that change their management style and philosophy to match the last great management author they read. They quote them, as though they were the last word on the subject. Don't get me wrong, I strongly recommend reading books on management as it is a way of assisting one in maintaining their own executive style.

Beware of the fad management books that claim to have the answers to the manager's dilemmas through the use of some model or series of pithy statements. Some of the best management books are well researched biographies of great people.

You read these experiential encounters and take note of the way they handled management affairs. I once spent a week with Dwight Eisenhower and another week with U.S. Grant and another with Abraham Lincoln during the American Civil War in well written biographies, that included letters and reports that explained their thinking during times when great leadership and management was needed.

One may become a disciple of their particular discipline and practice what they have learned. A disciple is one who religiously engages in a disciplined study of a field of study including its doctrines. A disciple can be one who faithfully studies the doctrines of another who has forwarded a field of study. A disciple is one who recognizes the validity of the doctrine then defends the accuracy of the doctrine and assists in spreading that doctrine.

A discipline is a field of study formulated on specific principles or theories with corresponding methods for proving those principles and theories actually prove the relevance of the field of study. Mathematics is a discipline as is physics and Psychology. Discipline also means the maintenance of pre-established standards. A field of study has established standards on which to measure the validity and effectiveness of the discipline.

The body of principles and theories that form the foundation of a specific discipline make up the doctrines of that discipline. A doctrine or doctrines of a discipline includes a system of beliefs a philosophy of thought and a statement of fundamental policies that govern the validity and continuity of the field of study. It usually includes methods for proving the validity of the theories used to formulate the doctrine. To be a disciple of a doctrine first requires one to vigorously engage in disciplined research and study of the doctrine in order to understand it, to grasp and comprehend how that doctrine relates to life in general and other disciplines then agree and accept those precepts to be true.

A disciple *of* one who has formulated or champions a specific doctrine will willingly indulge in a learning about that champion through cognitive penetration of a searching mind that will go beyond the obvious or superfluous and establishing such a thorough understanding as to how and why the champion has come to the conclusions they have published. You will notice that a disciple is continuously engaged in a better understanding the field of study and the consequent doctrine.

In this thesis I have shown that a disciple of a legitimate field of study is actively, continuously indulged in it and normally becomes an expert in the field capable of teaching others.

In the field of Industrial and Organizational Psychology there are those who have made substantial contributions to the field through research and published works. Some call them Gurus but those champions of the science call themselves students or disciples of the discipline. There are those who religiously follow the careers of these people and cling to their every word.

In the 1970s through the 1990s there were two undisputed experts in the field of I/O Psych; Number one was Don Kirkpatrick and the number two expert was C.P. Campbell. I did some post graduate work with Kirkpatrick at the University of Wisconsin in Madison. I took several classes from C.P. Campbell in the University of Tennessee in Knoxville. They were true innovators in the field of Industrial Psychology.

In those days and even today when you attend an Industrial & Organizational conference you will hear people say they are disciples of Don Kirkpatrick or C. P. Campbell. The unique thing about these people who call themselves disciples of these professors is that they know more about the person than the material they published.

I suppose that in any field of study there are devout disciples and peripheral disciples. There are other professors and students of the field that have published theories and practices they claim are effective methods of organizational development. I have read many of them and I can tell you there are a lot of charlatans who have a following. Those of whom I speak have never broken sweat in a manufacturing setting. There are those who have formulated methods for measuring OD initiatives that work, but are so narrowly focused they are practically meaningless.

The great ones in my field have published theories and practical methods that have revolutionized the field. And because of this they sell everything they published and sold out venues when they gave personal appearance speeches. I have studied what the greats of my field wrote and I have learned about them. I have sat in on their lectures and many I have met personally.

One major thing I discovered about these great men and women was they were more reputation than substance. More often than not their contribution was limited to one or just a few discoveries but their disciples would hang on their every word as if everything they said was handed down from the mountain.

More often than not once they moved past their signature contribution they had nothing more to offer than what was already published. Their disciples awarded them accolades they did not earn and gave them credit for quotes they did not say. Too often another student on the field of I/O would take the great one's idea and expand it to make it more useable, but the credit for this expansion still went to the great ones.

Here is a key element of discipleship. A true disciple learns more than they have been taught and they share that knowledge with others in the field.

I have witnessed trusted teachers who once taught faithful stewardship, pragmatic management and capitalism convert to socialistic and liberal philosophies and have weakened the integrity of the organization and its ability to remain sea-worthy. And to those young men and women who have plans to enter the management field as a business executive of military officer and are seeking knowledge and wisdom from the great management authors of the time.

Don't be fooled by glib philosophical statements about sharing leadership when they really mean sharing command.

The one in charge must be in charge, the people that report to you expect you to be the last word. You will recall on page 94 the interviewer then asked coach Bear Bryant; how he handled strong willed coaches. He asked; "How does that work, strength against strength?" Coach Paul "Bear" Bryant responded by saying; "Its not strength against strength. I'm the boss! I listen to them and I incorporate things they say into the plan if it's the right thing to do at the time, but when they walk away they go to carry out my plan, my orders, they do it my way, because I am ultimately responsible. Whether it works out well or not, it is my responsibility.

I have heard many of the published gurus providing advice that sound good in the classroom. The real test is if those theories work on the production floor.

One who expects to be a successful corporate executive must learn more than they were taught. The new executive must establish their own unique style, their own philosophies, management axioms and rules of command. Once established they we must be consistent in the application of them. We can change our ideas when we find a more applicable method of management, but we do not abandon them and try on another just because a well worded or well written piece seems to make sense. We test it we examine it and abandon it or adopt portions of it, if it meets with our own beliefs and experience.

The best text book is your own experience. You pay attention, to how other managers do things or think through things you take notes and you test those means to determine from your own or your vicarious experiences if they are applicable to you and your management style. Captain Mills explained it very succinctly to Mr. McCormick; "Mr. McCormick, everyone who becomes a ship's captain brings to that job his own philosophy of command. That philosophy is the sum total of everything he's read, seen, heard or thought. We read textbooks on leadership, we've sat through lectures and seminars on command, watched our superiors succeed or fail by their actions, and observed our own attempts turn out well or poorly. Through all these experiences, we've each developed our own thoughts and ideas concerning the proper way to command a ship".

The ship and the crew were so steeped in a status-quo, don't rock the boat mentality that only a major test of skill, material and equipment would wake them out of their stupor, and that is exactly what Captain Mills did.

He took them out and watched them fail. They learned from their failure and they took advantage of his opportunity to prepare themselves and to do it again.

This time they succeeded, in spite of the unforeseen problem of getting out of channel. Overcoming that obstacle was another test they passed and it added to their self respect.

As for letting Mister Winthrop melt down during the trip through the auxiliary channel It is a risk anytime a leader allows a high level subordinate to make a fool of himself in front of lower level managers and employees, but sometimes it is a risk that needs to be taken. In almost every situation, the senior manager will take steps to protect a high level subordinate from embarrassing the management team but this was not a normal situation.

The captain allowed Mr. Winthrop to crash and burn in front of the entire ship's company. He had to allow his credibility to diminish to the point that he would no longer influence the officers and the crew. Circumstances, or a clever plan, put Mr. Winthrop in a situation where only the captain could save him, or let him sink.

I have personally witnessed a once valuable subordinate try to usurp power. In one case the senior smashed the upstart like a bug, with humiliation and a ruthless termination. That put fear in the hearts of the entire company and no one ever tried that again. In another case, the senior saved the maverick and won the loyalty of that executive and all who witnessed it, forever thereafter.

The Captain saved Mister Winthrop's career. It was not easy task but he persevered until he found away. Not because he feared the Royal Winthrop's, but because it was the right thing to do for a person with John Winthrop's potential.

Rule of Command # 14
When it is in your power to do good or withhold good, never withhold good.

Management Axiom:

Only you can be you. Establish your own management style, set your own management axioms, your own rules of command based on what works for you, not something that may work for someone else.
Not all great men are wise!

A true professional learns more than they have been taught and they share that knowledge with others in the field.

Handling Talent and Temperament

It is not unusual to find brilliant persons, and highly skilled or specifically trained individuals with unusual quirks. It is not unusual to find professionals, such as accountants, purchasing managers, sales representatives, scientists and computer types with unique world views and personal character traits that fall outside the norm (whatever norm is).

Many executives who have had to grapple their way to high positions are very turf conscious and jealously cling to their own ideas when it comes to assessing their departments, or their way of managing their departments. Talent comes with temperament and the effective manager learns how to deal with the temperament, because in the long run these "strange ducks" are usually substantial contributors to the organization's welfare.

Some of the most consistent and mellow performers are those who have developed a maturity from a personal standpoint first, and based on that, they mold a professional maturity that earns credibility and recognition from all who do business with these people. These people will, over time, consistently out-perform the highly educated and those with I.Q.s in the bright and brilliant range.

Management Axiom:

The executive should do whatever it takes to avoid surprises. If you are not sure a certain plan will produce expected outcomes, think it through or practice it.

Professional competence and personal maturity will outclass and outperform I.Q. in the long run.

Postlude:

The problem Captain Mills met when he first came aboard was that the officers and crew had lost commitment to the organization and its mission. His first task was to rebuild that commitment, by showing them it was worthwhile, attainable and they had it within them to bring it about. It was not the incompetence of his officers or senior enlisted, that brought about the current condition, it was that they were not willing to assume responsibility of command. They were afraid of jeopardizing their positions by making a mistake. They needed someone who would *take the bullet* until they could gain the confidence in themselves and their ship mates to take initiative and issue orders according to their own judgment.

The captain intended to empower his officers to take charge of their own areas of responsibility by giving them the opportunity to achieve what they were there to achieve. He provided a written plan on which to base their actions. He guided them along this charted course by using suggestions, recommendations, persuasion and persistent follow-up. When results were not as forthcoming as it needed to be in order to meet the Gitmo deadline he moved into his stateroom in order to be right in the action at all times. He was their captain not just their chief executive. He constantly reminded them of his vision for the ship, its officers and crew. He continually reaffirmed it and asserted it until each officer and enlisted bought into it and committed to it. They had to accept and implement the plans that would crystallize the vision and make it their own whole heartedly.

He brought them to a point of no return. They had come to grips with their own weaknesses. Like a personal athletic trainer he provided the means to strengthen themselves for greater tasks, tasks that provided evidence of Can Do. Once they gained that confidence in themselves, in their shipmates and the ship itself, they were ready to make the discussion and take the action necessary for performance. Now they are ready for the ultimate test. The combat readiness exercises in Guantanamo Bay Cuba.

Wade Johnson's 14 Rules of Command:

Rule of Command #1
Taking command requires getting others to think of you as the boss.

Rule of Command #2
When you are in charge, take charge.

Rule of Command #3
There is always a cause that prompts every action. Find and eliminate the causes of misconduct and poor performance.

Rule of Command #4
Do not delay taking disciplinary action, whether to correct or reward. The longer you wait the less impact it will have.

Rule of Command #5
When you have tried everything and cooperation cannot be attained, require compliance with consequences for failure to comply.

Rule of Command #6
Management is a contest of wills, persistence is essential if one is to prevail.

Rule of Command #7
To get respect you must be respectable and give respect.

Rule of Command #8
In the final analysis the subordinate manager must be able to get results on their own, using their own methods.

Rule of Command #9
Never show fear in the face of difficult situations, never show defeat in the face of failure.

Rule of Command # 10
Maintain *pertinacity*. In situations where disaster is the consequence for continuing current practices, the executive must place one action before all others and insist on a successful outcome.

Rule of Command #11
Never, never, never surprise the boss!

Rule of Command #12
Your most significant responsibility is creating an environment for individual opportunity. Reward those who embrace it, replace those who do not.

Rule of Command #13:
You do not owe anyone a job, they can't handle. It is better to leave a position vacant than to give it to someone who cannot handle it or who just will not fit in.

Rule of Command # 14
When it is in your power to do good or withhold good, never withhold good.

Post Script

One never knows how they may influence the lives of others. Perhaps if one exercised more selflessness and less selfishness there would be more joy in the world.

Appendix

The Captain

"Only a seaman realizes to what great extent an entire ship reflects the personality and ability of one individual, her Commanding Officer. To a landsman this is not understandable and sometimes it is even difficult for us to understand. But it is so!

A ship at sea is a distinct world in herself and in consideration of the protracted and distant operations of fleet units, the Navy must place great power, responsibility and trust in the hands of those leaders chosen for command.

In each ship there is one man who, in the hour of emergency or peril at sea, can turn to no other man. There is one who ultimately is responsible for the safe navigation, engineering performance, accurate gunfire, and morale of his ship. He is the Commanding Officer. He is the ship.

This is the most difficult and demanding assignment in the Navy. There is not an instant during his tour as Commanding Officer that he can escape the grasp of command responsibility. His privileges in view of his obligations are almost ludicrously small; nevertheless Command is the spur that has given the Navy its great leaders.

It is a duty that most richly deserves the highest, time-honored title of the seafaring world ... CAPTAIN.'

Joseph Conrad

Psalms 107: 123-128

They that go down to the sea in ships, that do business in great waters;

These see the works of the Lord, and his wonders in the deep.
For He commands, and raises the stormy wind, which lifted up the waves.

They mount up to the heaven, they go down again to the depths; their soul is melted because of trouble.

They reel to and fro, and stagger like a drunken man, at their wit's end.

Then they cry unto the Lord in their trouble, and he brings them out of their distresses.

The Navy Hymn

Eternal Father, strong to save, whose arm hath bound the restless wave, Who bids the mighty ocean deep Its own appointed limits keep;

Oh, hear us when we cry to Thee, for those in peril on the sea!

O Christ! Whose voice the waters heard and hushed their raging at Thy word, who walked on the foaming deep, And calm amidst its rage didst sleep;

Oh, hear us when we cry to Thee, for those in peril on the sea!

Most Holy Spirit! Who didst brood upon the chaos dark and rude and bid its angry tumult cease, and give, for wild confusion, peace;

Oh, hear us when we cry to Thee, for those in peril on the sea!

O Master of love and power! Our brethren shield in danger's hour; From rock and tempest, fire and foe, protect them wheresoe'er they go;

Thus evermore shall rise to Thee Glad hymns of praise from land and sea.

While US Navy Ships go by the actual time on board the ship. Most official business is measured in Greenwich Mean Time (GMT) or in the communications section, Zulu Time. All military time is a 24 hour day as follows;

0000 Zero, zero, zero	Beginning the day	1300 Thirteen hundred	1 PM
0100 Zero one Hundred	1 AM	1400 Fourteen hundred	2 PM
0200 Zero two Hundred	2 AM	1500 Fifteen hundred	3 PM
0300 Zero three Hundred	3 AM	1600 Sixteen hundred	4 PM
0400 Zero four Hundred	4 AM	1700 Seventeen hundred	5 PM
0500 Zero five Hundred	5 AM	1800 Eighteen hundred	6 PM
0600 Zero six Hundred	6 AM	1900 Nineteen hundred	7 PM
0700 Zero seven Hundred	7 AM	2000 Twenty hundred	8 PM
0800 Zero eight Hundred	8 AM	2100 Twenty one hundred	9 PM
0900 Zero nine Hundred	9 AM	2200 Twenty two hundred	10 PM
1000 Ten Hundred	10 AM	2300 Twenty three hundred	11 PM
1100 Eleven Hundred	11 AM	2359 Twenty three fifty nine	Midnight
1200 Twelve Hundred	12 Noon		There is no 2400

A commissioned US Navy ship, including ready reserves can never be left unattended. At *minimum of one-third of the assigned crew must be on board at all times. The auxiliary equipment must be fired up at all times, especially the electricity and water supplies. Of course it is axiomatic that all vital equipment on board must be under guard. Shipboard* routine, whether in port or at sea, is a 24 hour seven days a week operation. Work duties are divided into watches of four hours at a time, except the dog watches which are two hours.

000-0400	Mid Watch
0400-0800	Morning Watch
0800-1200	Forenoon Watch
1200-1600	Afternoon Watch
1600-1800	First Dog Watch (two hours)
1800-2000	Second Dog Watch (two Hours)
2000-2359	First Watch

Ships Bells are struck from reveille to taps except during divine services, or when the ship is darkened, for security reasons or when the fog signal is being sounded. The bell informs watch standers the time of watch.

Hours of watch		Bells	Rings (Strikes)
0030	First half-hour bell	One	*
0100	First hour	Two	**
0130	First hour and half	Three	** *
0200	Second hour	Four	** **
0230	Second hour and half	Five	** ** *
0300	Third hour	Six	** ** **
0330	Third hour and half	Seven	** ** ** *
0400	Fourth hour	Eight	** ** ** **

Glossary of Naval Terms

1MC	The basic one-way communications system on a vessel. Reaches all spaces on a ship. Used for general announcements, and to transmit general alarm system signals. Control stations are located on the bridge, quarterdeck, and central station. Other transmitters may be installed at additional points. There are other MC and JV circuits used for communications within the ship. They are typically system-specific, i.e. weapons systems, navigation communication, engineering systems, firefighting, etc.
Aft	Near the stern
After	That which is furtherest aft
Admiral one star	Naval Officer Rank 07 Rear Admiral lower half - equal to Army Brigadier General
Admiral two stars	Naval Officer Rank 08 Rear Admiral upper half - equal to Army Major General
Admiral three stars	Naval Officer Rank 09 Vice Admiral - equal to Army Lieutenant General
Admiral four stars	Naval Officer Rank 10 Admiral - equal to Army General
Admiral five stars	Naval Officer Rank 11 Fleet Admiral (used in wartime only) Army five star generals (used only in wartime)
All Hands	All ship's company no exceptions
Ashcan	A depth charge which is cylindrical in shape
Astern	Directly behind the ship
Aweigh	Anchor is clear of the bottom and the ship is underway
Aye, Aye	Reply to a command or order, to acknowledge understanding of the meaning
AWOL Bag	Overnight bag sailors take with them on liberty
Belay	Disregard, discontinue, or stop current action
Between the Devil and the Deep	In wooden ships, the "devil" was the longest seam in the hull of the ship. It ran from the bow to the stern. When at sea and the "devil" had to be caulked, the sailor sat in a bo'sun's chair to do so. He was suspended between the "devil" and the sea — the "deep" — a very precarious position, especially when the ship was underway.
Boatswain (boat – son)	Officer, usually a warrant officer or a chief in charge of the deck.
Boatswain's mate	Enlisted person responsible for various duties pertaining to the deck
Bogey	Unidentified air contact. May turn out to be friendly, neutral, or hostile.
Bridge	Area of the superstructure from which the ship is operated (Conn)
Bug Juice	Kool Aid
Bulkhead	Vertical partition in a ship (wall but never called a wall)

BuPers	Bureau of Personnel.(Naval Human Resources and assignments)
BuShips	Bureau of Ships. Navy department responsible for the accounting for and repair of ships in the US navy.
Cabin	Living compartment for the ship's commanding officer
Captain	The chief executive officer plenipotentiary on board a sea going vessel. Also Naval officer Rank O-6 equal to Colonel in the Army
Carry on	Order to resume previous activity after interruption
Chain of Command	The succession from superior to subordinate through which command is exercised.
Chart	Nautical counterpart of a road map, showing land configurations, water depths and aids to navigation
Colors	The national ensign; the ceremony of raising and lowering the ensign
ComDesDiv	Commander Destroyer Division
ComDesRon	Commander Destroyer Squadron
Commander	Naval officer rank O-5 equal to Lt. Colonel in Army
Companionway	Opening in the deck giving access to a ladder for going up or down
ComResDesDiv	Commander Reserve Destroyer Division
ComResDesRon	Commander Reserve Destroyer Squadron
Conn	In charge of or controlling the ships seagoing operations while underway
Course	The ship's desired direction of travel, not to be confused with heading
Coxswain	(kock-son) Enlisted person in charge of a boat usually acts as a helmsman.
Crow's Nest	The raven, or crow, was an essential part of the Vikings' navigation equipment. These land-lubbing birds were carried on aboard to help the ship's navigator determine where the closest land lay when weather prevented sighting the shore. In cases of poor visibility, a crow was released and the navigator plotted a course corresponding to the bird's flight path because the crow invariably headed towards land. The Norsemen carried the birds in a cage secured to the top of the mast. Later on, as ships grew and the lookout stood his watch in a tub located high on the main mast, the name "crow's nest" was given to this tub. While today's Navy still uses lookouts in addition to radars, etc., the crow's nest is a thing of the past.
Cut of her	Actually cut of the jib. From the days of sail, when individual sails were made aboard the ship and a certain amount of individuality was expressed in the design (shape and size) of the sails. Now it is the shape and size of the ship and its superstructure. Ships could be, and were, identified by the "cut of their jib."
Davy Jones Davy Jones' Locker	The bottom of the sea.
Dead ahead	Directly ahead; relative bearing of 000 degrees
Dead astern	Directly behind the ship 180 degrees relative
Dead in the water	Complete loss of all power resulting in no propulsion and no steering. Adrift, vulnerable to the elements and the sea.

Deck	Horizontal planking or plating that divides a ship into layers (floors - but never called floors)
DD	Destroyer – Ships before 1970 were small ships with two stacks
DE	Destroyer Escort – Small ships with one stack usually 310-306 feet long anti-submarine warfare responsibilities.
DER	Destroyer Escort with sophisticated radar systems mounted on the mast for ASW, Radar & AA defense.
Dock	Space alongside a pier where ships are tied
Dogwatch	A dogwatch at sea is the period between 4 and 6 p.m., the first dogwatch, or the period between 6 and 8 p.m., the second dogwatch. The dogwatches are only two hours each so the same Sailors aren't always on duty at the same time each afternoon. Some experts say dogwatch is a corruption of dodge watch and others associate dogwatch with the fitful sleep of Sailors called dog sleep, because it is a stressful watch. But no one really knows the origin of this term, which was in use at least back to the 1700s.
Eight Bells	Aboard Navy ships, bells are struck to designate the hours of being on watch. Each watch is four hours in length. One bell is struck after the first half-hour has passed, two bells after one hour has passed, three bells after an hour and a half, four bells after two hours, and so forth up to eight bells are struck at the completion of the four hours. Completing a watch with no incidents to report was "Eight bells and all is well." The practice of using bells stems from the days of the sailing ships. Sailors couldn't afford to have their own time pieces and relied on the ship's bells to tell time. The ship's boy kept time by using a half-hour glass. Each time the sand ran out, he would turn the glass over and ring the appropriate number of bells.
Eight O'clock reports	Reports received by the executive officer from departmental heads at 2000 (twenty hundred 8 PM).
Ensign	The national flag or the lower grade of a naval commissioned officer equal to a second miss in the Army.
Executive Officer	Second officer in Command. Chief Operating Officer.
Fantail	The after end of the main deck
Fathom	Unit of depth equal to 6 feet.
First Lieutenant	(USN) Deck Division officer aboard ship, or officer responsible for general seamanship and deck evolutions. Generally the deck department head. As used, it's an assignment, not a rank.
Flank Speed	Top Speed.
Fleet	An organization of ships, aircraft, marine forces, and shore-based fleet activities, all under one commander, for conducting major operations.
Fore and Aft	The entire length of the ship.
Forecastle – (fok-sul)	Forward section of the main deck, generally extending from the stem aft to just about the anchor windlass.
Galley	Space where food is prepared (kitchen, but not called kitchen).
Gangway	More properly called a "brow," the temporary bridge connecting the ship's quarterdeck to the pier. (2) A call to get out of the way, which originated as a call for junior personnel to give precedence to a senior while crossing the gangway.

Gedunk / Geedunk	(1) Dessert/junk food/candy, or a place to buy same. Aka 'pogey bait'. (2) "Extras" or benefits, awards, ribbons, or medals. (3) Easy or "sweet" duty. Can be used as noun or verb. "Gedunk" may be a corruption of the German "ge tunk which means to repetitively dip something. Gedunk apparently was first used specifically to refer to ice cream sodas.
GQ	General Quarters – A condition of full readiness for battle.
GQ alarm	An alarm that sends all hands to their designated battle stations.
Head	Toilet. The 'head' on a sailing ship is located all the way forward, where the figurehead was attached to the hull. Thus, the name arrived from the figurehead on the sailing ship. On either side of the bowsprit next to the figurehead, the crew could relieve themselves.
Heading	The direction toward which the ship's bow is pointing at any instant.
Heave to	To stop or reduce headway just enough to maintain steerageway.
Helm	Mechanical device used to turn the rudder (usually a wheel aboard ship, a lever in boats).
Helmsman	A person who steers the ship by turning her helm (also called steersman).
Knee Knockers	The coaming of a watertight door or bulkhead opening. These coamings are a foot or so off the deck. So called because they can wreak havoc on the shins of those new to shipboard life.
Knot	Nautical miles per hour. Knot = 6,076.10 ft. per hour or 1.5 miles per hour.
Ladder	Shipboard flight of stairs.
Lee	An area sheltered from the wind, downwind, the side of the ship not receiving sea or wind
Lieutenant	Officer Rank O-3 equal to Captain in Army.
Lieutenant Commander	Naval Officer Rank O-4 equal to Major in the Army.
Lieutenant Junior Grade (jg)	Officer Rank 0-2 Equal to a First miss in the Army.
Log	A complete daily record, by watches in which is described every circumstance or occurrence of importance or interest hour by hour
Mail Buoy Watch	A practical joke pulled on inexperienced crewmembers and midshipmen which revolves around convincing the victim that mail is delivered to a ship at sea via a buoy.
Main Deck	The upper most complete deck.
Mate	Another sailor.
Midrats	Food served at midnight for ongoing watch standers, although the oncoming watch section commonly does not get up early enough to partake. Off-going section gets the remnants, if any. Usually a combination of leftovers, plus something new to round out the service. A contraction of "midnight rations."
Mooring Line	Lines used to tie the ship to the pier or to another ship. Mooring lines are numbered from forward aft; the direction they tend (lead) is also sometimes given. 'Number one mooring line' typically is made fast at the bow, and tends straight across to the pier or other ship. Spring lines tend forward or aft of their attachment point.

Mustang	An officer promoted from enlisted ranks and received a commission
NavBase	Naval Base. The actual command that houses several operational departments and naval stations.
NavSta	Naval Station.
NROTC	Naval Reserve Officer Training Command - a college program that trains college students to be officers in the Navy. They receive a commission at graduation.
Overhead	Underside of a deck which forms the overhead of a compartment (ceiling but never called a ceiling).
Passageway	A corridor used for interior horizontal movement aboard ship.
Petty Officer	Non Commissioned Officer E-4 to E-9 equal to Corporal to sergeant status in the army.
Pier	Structure extending from land into the water to provide a mooring for vessels
Pipe	To sound a particular call on a boatswain's pipe.
Plan of the Day	Schedule of a day's routine and events ordered by the executive officer and published daily aboard ship or at a shore activity.
Port	To the left of the centerline of the ship when facing forward.
Quarterdeck	Deck designated by the commanding officer as the place to carry out official functions; station of the officer of the deck while the ship is in port.
Quartermaster	Naval rating charged with navigation-related duties.
Ring Knocker	A Naval Academy Graduate that constantly reminds others of his pedigree .
Running lights	Navigational lights shown at night by a vessel under way.
Sea Anchor	A device for holding it end-on to the sea.
Seamanship	Skill in the use of deck equipment, in boat handling.
Secure	To make "fast" to stop or cease from an activity, to make an area off limits for general use
Scuttle	The deliberate sinking of one's own ship.
Scuttlebutt	Rumors about the goings on aboard ship. Usually the information is correct. Deriving from the nautical term for the cask used to serve water (or, later, a water fountain conventionally stored in a **scuttled butt**: A butt (cask) which had been scuttled by making a hole in it so the water could be withdrawn.
Shake down	A rigorous series of events designed to train crew for some activity and/or to discover problems with the ship in order make corrections.
Ship's Company	All hands permanently assigned to a ship or station.
Sound	To determine the depth of water.
Sound Powered Phones	Phone system powered by voice of user.
Special Sea and Anchor Detail	Crew assigned special duties when leaving or entering port.
Squadron	Two or more divisions of ships or aircraft.
Square	To make things right, to ensure a proper relationship.
Square away	To make shipshape, to put in proper order.
Stack	Shipboard chimney.

Stanchion	Vertical posts for supporting decks, smaller, similar posts for supporting lifelines or awnings.
Starboard	Direction to the right of the centerline as one faces forward.
State Room	A living compartment for an officer or officers.
Stem	Extreme forward line of the bow.
Stern	The aftermost part of the vessel.
Superstructure	The structure above a ship's main deck
Swab	Mop (slang for enlisted sailor).
Wardroom	Officers messing and meeting compartment.
Watch	One of the periods, usually 4 hours, into which a day is divided.
Weather deck	Any deck exposed to the elements (weather).
White hat	Slang for enlisted sailors. The hat worn by enlisted Navy
Windward	In the direction of the wind – The side of the ship being hit by wind, weather, and sea.
X-Ray	Damage control material condition – Personnel remain at General Quarters until condition is secured.
Zebra	Damage Control material condition (a grave battle condition).

If you enjoyed this book, you will like the follow up book in the Stewardship of Management Series:

Stewardship of Command:
Managing in Turbulent times
ISBN-13: 978-1456557324   ISBN-10: 1456557327

You may also ejoy the Novel that was extrapolated from this series:

USS CARD
ISBN - 13:978-1466314429 ISBN – 10:1466314427 Copyright 2011

Made in the USA
Columbia, SC
07 April 2023